Mr. Blackwell's

WORST:

30 YEARS OF FASHION FIASCOS

MR. BLACKWELL
with
VERNON PATTERSON

PHAROS BOOKS
A SCRIPPS HOWARD COMPANY

NEW YORK

Copyright © 1991 by Mr. Blackwell

All rights reserved.

No part of this book may be reproduced in any form or by any means without permission in writing from the publisher.

First published in 1991.

Library of Congress Cataloging-in-Publication Data

Blackwell, Mr.

**Mr. Blackwell's worst :
30 years of fashion fiascos**

Mr. Blackwell with Vernon Patterson.

p. cm.

Includes index.

ISBN 0-88687-625-7 : $14.95

1. Fashion–History–20th century. 2. Celebrities.
I. Patterson, Vernon. II. Title.

GT596.B55 1991   91-11106

391'.009'045–dc20   CIP

Printed in the United States of America

Cover design by Douglas & Voss Group
Interior design by Rich Sheinaus / Gotham Design

Pharos Books
A Scripps Howard Company
200 Park Avenue
New York, NY 10166

10 9 8 7 6 5 4 3 2 1

Pharos Books are available at special discounts
on bulk purchases for sales promotions, premiums,
fundraising or educational use.
For details, contact the Special Sales Department,
Pharos Books, 200 Park Avenue,
New York, NY 10166.

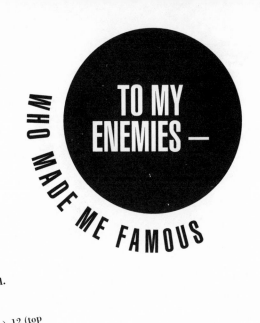

TO MY ENEMIES — WHO MADE ME FAMOUS

CON TENTS

WORST:

Fiascos

1

FOR THE PAST THIRTY YEARS, THE ANNUAL WORST Dressed List has been something of a cause célèbre among fashion victims, Seventh Avenue, the American public, and the world at large. For three decades I've chronicled the fashion flops, frumps, and fiascos . . . and I've learned that bad fashion, like bad credit, is eternal. The timeless trend toward the tacky and terrible is omnipotent . . . and no one is above or beyond a Blackwell bashing if she truly deserves it. The most famous, fawned over, and fabulous women in the world have starred in the annual annihilation; in fact, the ladies who make The List cover the fashion waterfront from actresses to singers to socialites – with a few gender-benders in between.

During the past three decades, fashion has drastically changed – styles have evolved, heated up, sold out, cooled down, burned out . . . and finally died. Like fashion itself, some of the most illustrious ladies on my list have faded into oblivion while others have maintained their stardom – in spite of their horrendous taste – for more years than anyone cares to remember.

It all began quite innocently. In 1960, I was asked by *American Weekly*, an insert magazine in Sunday newspapers across the country, to write a piece on Hollywood's worst and best dressed – never expecting the public explosion that followed. As a designer, I found that the overpampered, overpuffed, overperfumed, over-publicized and overdressed ladies of the silver screen knew as much about fashion as King Kong . . . and said so. But I always kept my idol-bashing on a fashion level: personalities, performances, and/or

backstage tantrums didn't interest me – their closets did, the
contents of which were in need
of an immediate fashion fix
or a complete overhaul.

Much to my surprise,
people listened, looked, and –
thank God – laughed. Because even
though I abhorred fashion slavery, I delivered my
gibes with tongue firmly in cheek. People were shocked.
People were amused. People were relieved that someone had the
nerve to say out loud what, in truth, they had been thinking for
years. And, so, The List was born . . . a list I fully expected to last a
season at the very most. Little did I suspect I would still be wreaking
havoc on a seething Seventh Avenue thirty years later. Some say it's
a dirty job, but somebody's gotta do it. It might as well be me.

If it's true that one can tell more about a society by its failures
than its successes, then at least on a fashion level, this book is a
revelation. And if the following pages do have an underlying
message, it's one of fashion individuality. Reject false fashion
images, Madison Avenue's latest advertising blitz, and what's
considered "in" and "out." Say no to the outrageous demands of the
fashion potentates who scheme up new looks to fill their coffers. The
female body is a work of art to be glorified, not desecrated.

I'm not implying that there are no great designers working
today. On the contrary, evergreen collections of Chanel, Givenchy,

Left to Right:

Mr. Blackwell
with Jane Russell,
Julie Christie,
Zsa Zsa Gabor,
Jayne Mansfield

Above:

*The young
Mr. Blackwell.*

St. Laurent, Dior, and Trigère are wonders to behold. But even a slinky St. Laurent on the wrong woman can spell fashion flop. Let's face it: a burlap bag would look good on Audrey Hepburn or Catherine Deneuve . . . but all of us are not Audrey or Catherine clones, which brings us back to discussing thirty years of Blackwell's Worst. Truth is certainly stranger than fiction; not even Edgar Allan Poe could have imagined the visions of terror I've witnessed.

In fact, who could believe a Cher? An Elizabeth Taylor? A Barbra Streisand? A Madonna? Only a fashion masochist experiencing a dreadful fever dream under a full moon, that's for sure, which proves that you can be famous, rich, powerful, talented, and gorgeous – and still look like something the cat refuses to drag in. That's why The List has always stressed celebrities: these people have no excuse. Needless to say, I hit a few Hollywood nerves over the years. Some were angry, some said they didn't give a damn, but most – in a strange, back-handed way – were flattered.

They knew it was all done in campy fun, despite the unfortunate truth involved. The international publicity didn't hurt, either. Of course, their fans erupted in protests and the press had a fashion field day. Still, what otherwise could have been a very dry season for many of the Listmakers suddenly turned into a veritable monsoon of publicity. Most only got really angry when they were taken off – like Whoopi Goldberg and Lynn Redgrave. The turnaround was amazing. Appearing on The List became a retro

"No good deed goes unpunished."
—Anonymous

Above:

Mr. Blackwell
checking over
his list.

status symbol – kind of like being on Nixon's enemies list. Everyone pretended to be surprised, but many were secretly thrilled. The public loved the idea because they told me so. So did the media. If imitation is the sincerest form of flattery, then I'll admit to feeling a bit satisfied. For better or worse, The List has managed to spawn a stream of copycat compilations, most of which faded into oblivion because of their boring seriousness about a truly hilarious spectacle. Seeing Nancy Reagan in knickers is cause for laughter. It's either that – or lose your mind completely.

I haven't lost my mind – yet. Even after all these years of witnessing fashion debacles that make the sinking of the Titanic look like a week at Disneyland, I've tried to maintain a sense of humor about it all. Because in the long run, we're not talking about inventing the atom bomb. What The List does, on some sort of sequined level, is to chronicle pop culture, comment on current trends, poke fun at pomposity, ridicule arrogance, and point the finger at the ones who deserve it most. God knows, they made The List the old-fashioned way: they earned it, with every polyester pantsuit, every psychedelic halter top, every Miami Venus gold lamé bathing suit thrust our unsuspecting way. And now it's time to take a look at these symbols of fashion frivolity. It's thirty years of the worst . . . so proceed at your own risk.

1960

AS WE ENTERED A NEW decade, fashion was rapidly evolving from the vapid, girl-next-door, professional virgin-for-life looks made popular by Sandra Dee, Doris Day, and Debbie Reynolds. As the sixties burst into view, so, too, did bustlines, most notably from the likes of Monroe and Mansfield – cartoon cutouts for the lusty American male. Suddenly, curvaceous, sultry, and skin tight were in and grew even more popular as the years and morals progressed or digressed – I can't quite figure out which. The attempts by nearly everyone in fashion to reject the tame, tired, and timid fashions of the fifties caused a lot of split hems and pushup bras to wreak havoc on the American woman. In 1960, this influence was just beginning to occur. For the most part, 1960 saw a plethora of princess silhouettes, culottes, divided skirts, and, for evening, the obligatory beaded evening dress – preferably short. Sweeping coats were back in vogue, plaids and patterned fabrics were popular. Grape, bottle green, and plum were favorite hues, while the ultimate status symbol in 1960 was the leopard coat. My, how times have changed . . .

Anna Magnani

The female counterpart of Emmett Kelly. One of the most distinguished actresses of our generation, who suggests Eleanora Duse playing in a Shakespearean tragedy wearing tramp clothes.

1·9·6·0
2

Brigitte Bardot

An unruly child who has acquired the bad habit of taking off her nightie before the bathroom door has been closed.

1·9·6·0

③▶

Yvonne De Carlo

A gypsy who stole a wine-red portiere from a window and draped it over her body in combination with a Kelly green couch cover.

1960

Lucille Ball ·

1·9·6·0

④

One of our most gifted comediennes, she seems to bend over backwards to look ridiculous, and her greatest asset in this department is her clothes. Her preferences in fashion can best be described as a sense of turmoil, because nothing blends or complements.

1·9·6·0

⑤

Anita Ekberg

If a woman who wears a shoe two sizes too small is apt to suffer from bunions, I wonder what is the fate of one with a 39-inch bust who wears a size 16 dress? Miss Ekberg, in either street or formal wear, provokes the idea that she dresses with a shoehorn.

> *"You don't need nudity. A real actress should have her clothes on."*
> – 1960 LISTMAKER ANITA EKBERG
>
> *"It's obvious she never learned to act!"*
> – MR. BLACKWELL

7

1960

6

Shelley Winters

The only description for Miss Winters dressed for a party is a rag doll brought to the circus and covered with pink cotton candy.

7

Carolyn Jones

There is so little material between Miss Jones' bust line and the hem of her garment one wonders which will get where first.

8

Kim Novak

Lavender, like old lace, belongs in a bureau drawer, not on a torso with too great a frequency and without something complementary to offset it. She has adopted lavender as her trademark and is guilty of fabric redundancy.

My first list – in both the worst and best-dressed categories – named all established Hollywood stars. Later, I changed the formula to include political figures, singers, society matrons, and, on certain unavoidable occasions, men. But in 1960 *American Weekly* requested "the best and worst of Hollywood," thereby beginning the tradition of pointing the finger at the screen idols who should have known better but didn't. At this time, I could only come up with nine worst-dressed women. That's the last time that would ever happen. Ten was my number!

Shelley Winters had just won the Best Supporting Actress Oscar for *The Diary of Anne Frank.* "I couldn't decide whether to be dignified or sexy," she remarked after the show. Dressed in a boring, dark, dreary, off-the-shoulder gown accented with a string of pearls, Shelley was neither, but at least she still had her figure – a figure, I might add, that has grown in direct proportion with her reputation as an actress.

Bad dressers from foreign shores invaded America – and my list in 1960: Anna Magnani, direct from her tour de force in *The Rose Tattoo*; Brigitte Bardot, France's most intriguing export, and Anita Ekberg, Sweden's latest bombshell. They all proved dressing for disaster is an international prerogative.

Anne Baxter

1·9·6·0

She wears a sweater as if she were headed for the showers instead of a moonlight sail with a handsome escort. In formal attire her hair looks as if someone ran a brush through it and then said, "Oh the hell with it."

1961

IT WAS THE YEAR OF the beehive hairdo and the beginning of brand-new First Lady Jackie Kennedy's reign as the most famous woman of the fashion-conscious sixties, which she began with a stream of simple cloth coats, pillbox hats, and, for evening, elegant, simple-lined, bead-encrusted couturier confections from Paris. When she got in trouble for utilizing the genius of Givenchy instead of a suitable American counterpart, she switched to Oleg Cassini. Few noticed the difference since it was rumored she continued buying French fashion in secret and cut out all the labels. In other areas, 1961 saw the rise of the "little nothing" dress – with the big price tag – that enraptured high society, as did the "costume" look. Hats, shoes, handbags, coiffures, and even makeup were matched in style and color with accompanying dresses and coats. Too boring for mere words. Evening wear was more glamorous. Gold brocade, jeweled bodices, ruffled chiffon, silk and cut velvet were popular, while in Hollywood, the stuffed-sausage look, replete with exploding bustlines and split skirts, was getting out of control.

Worst 1 1961

Debbie Reynolds

If you're going to be a girl, go ahead and be one, but be one mentally. Debbie simply can't project the style she tries for in her clothes. They make her look silly.

Sophia Loren

Sophia Loren, off the screen, is still the Italian shop girl she portrays in the movies. Someone should tell her that simplicity is not drabness.

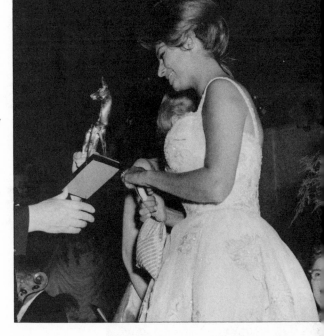

1·9·6·1
3
Marilyn Monroe

In private life, Marilyn Monroe is a road-show version of herself. She should get off the stage.

1·9·6·1
◁
4

Jayne Mansfield

Her plunging neckline has become a bare midriff problem.

> "Sex appeal is 50% what you've got and 50% what people think you've got."
> – 1961 LISTMAKER
> SOPHIA LOREN
>
> "Judging from the way she looked in 1961, I'd change thosepercentages to 30:70."
> – MR. BLACKWELL

1961

Lucille Ball

5

If you can't wear it, carry it. Lucy buys her clothes without any planning, then lugs around most everything else she owns. Her appearance is absolute confusion.

Zsa Zsa Gabor

1·9·6·1 **6**

Her arrogant independence in dressing makes her look like a clown.

1·9·6·1 **7**

Diana Dors

Nothing stylewise can be saved from this girl. Why bother?

1·9·6·1 **8**

Kathy Nolan

She dresses for the same role ("The Real McCoys") off camera, too. I can't understand it.

Connie Stevens

1·9·6·1 **9**

She wears anything she can get her hands on and it shows.

NOTES of INTEREST

In doing my lists I have very few regrets, but Miss Monroe's inclusion in 1961 was one, now that I look back on it. It was barely a year later that Marilyn would mysteriously leave us in what was, at the time, termed a suicide. Hollywood was in a state of shock for months and, in a way, still is. With the exception of Garbo, Marilyn Monroe just may have been the most enigmatic and legendary of all screen actresses.

Her imitators – Jayne Mansfield and Diana Dors – were in abundant states of undress throughout the year, and ended up, for the first and last time, in the same category Marilyn found herself in. At least I had the good sense to give Marilyn top billing over her clones. It was the least I could do.

After losing the Best Actress Oscar to ailing winner Elizabeth Taylor, Listmaker Shirley MacLaine was quoted as saying, "I lost to a tracheotomy." Her clothes were as tasteless as her one-liners.

Shirley MacLaine

Looks like everyone she knows has donated something to her wardrobe and she wears it all at the same time. In addition to this, she's a tomboy. She romps and rolls on the floor.

Zsa Zsa Gabor

Queen of the international set, she reminds me of the elephant in *Jumbo* with all its glittering trappings. Her outlandish entrances are a real farce.

Rosalind Russell

1·9·6·2

②

She's still Auntie Mame, and someone should remind her it was a comedy . . . slacks, bangles, headbands, and beads. Oh, please!

1962

1962 SYMBOLIZED A year of quiet but definite fashion changes. The silhouette became less abstract and more anatomical. The long evening coat returned as did the dinner suit, often in tweed or wool. The real fashion influences of 1962 were inspired by two wildly different actresses: Audrey Hepburn and Elizabeth Taylor.

The clothes Givenchy created for Miss Hepburn in the classic *Breakfast at Tiffany's* were credited with bringing in the vogue for the high-bosomed princess dresses without sleeves or belts. The style was perfect for Audrey – but disaster for anyone over size 6.

Film designer Irene Sharaff's Egyptian costumes for the upcoming epic *Cleopatra* starring Elizabeth Taylor and Richard Burton caused lots of excitement with the mummy and pyramid crowd. And Jackie Kennedy continued to make fashion news every time she stepped out of the White House in her modified Audrey Hepburn look.

I thought Mrs. Kennedy's knees were knobby and said so. The Oval Office was not amused.

1·9·6·2

3

Brigitte Bardot

A buxom milkmaid reminiscent of a cow wearing a girdle, and both have the same amount of acting talent.

1·9·6·2

4

Dinah Shore

She has tried every fashion at least once and still can't make up her mind. She's always Nashville's Little Miss Muffett, tossing kisses at a grade school pageant.

1·9·6·2

5

Judy Garland

Poor thing – apparently left all her fashionable clothes in that trunk she's always singing about.

1·9·6·2
Ingrid Bergman

If she has a brother Joe, he must have loaned her the clothes.

Oh No!

1·9·6·2
Bette Davis

Baby Jane's costumes aren't much different from the clothes I've seen her wearing around town.

NOTES of INTEREST

For two years in a row, the woman who made the word *Dahlink* an international affectation, Zsa Zsa Gabor, appeared on the list. Zsa Zsa, a good friend, laughed all the way to the jewelers. But another recipient of my dubious honor was not as pleased. In fact, Dinah Shore was livid.

Bette Davis took out ads in Hollywood trade papers looking for acting jobs. She should have spent her cash on a good dress, because when her next film, *Whatever Happened to Baby Jane?* opened, La Davis enjoyed a career resurgence to top 'em all – with the exception of Judy Garland, who had recently wowed New York at Carnegie Hall in what was dubbed "The Comeback of All Time."

Brigitte Bardot showed up again, as did Lucille Ball, proving something about the longevity of legendary fashion nightmares.

And Jackie Kennedy's sister-in-law, Pat Kennedy Lawford, didn't seem to possess an ounce of her family's glamour, but the worst was yet to come.

> *"The best time I ever had with Joan Crawford was when I pushed her down the stairs in Baby Jane."*
> – 1962 LISTMAKER BETTE DAVIS
>
> *"Bette was probably just a wee bit jealous that Crawford was infinitely better dressed."*
> – MR. BLACKWELL

Lucille Ball
1·9·6·2 **8**

Despite her great comedy flair, offstage she is a clown caricaturing an actress who borrowed her wardrobe from the studio costume department.

Mrs. Peter Lawford
1·9·6·2 **9**

She has absolutely no fashion image, and is drab and colorless, like a poor relative.

Laura Goldman
1·9·6·2 **10**

Neiman-Marcus Gown Buyer: From head to toe, her Tobacco Road ensembles (regardless of price) make her the number one nominee for my "I can't believe it!" list.

Zsa Zsa Gabor

Heading the list for the third year, Zsa Zsa Gabor is awarded lifetime membership in the Worst Dressed Club. I have your Golden Needle Award, Zsa Zsa, if you care to pick it up.

1·9·6·3 **②**

Elizabeth Taylor

Plunging neckline, deeper than should be legal; with plump bosoms, rounded hips, makes one think of the rebirth of the zeppelin.

"That son-of-a-bitch!" – 1963 Listmaker Elizabeth Taylor, after hearing of her Worst Dressed induction

"What can I say? The truth hurts!" – Mr. Blackwell

③

1·9·6·3

Shirley MacLaine

Basically basic – feathers and furs on her look like costumes borrowed from the Ziegfeld Follies.

1963

IT WAS THE YEAR OF Paul Newman's *Hud*, and the summer of Liz and Dick's *Cleopatra*.

Beverly Hills was sweltering under 100-degree heat and the pancake make-up was flowing faster than the Nile after monsoon season. Alfred Hitchcock's *The Birds* rattled a few cinematic cages while Peter, Paul and Mary's youth anthem, "Blowin' In The Wind," topped the charts.

Fashion was blowin' in the breeze of boredom; it seemed no one could decide what was in or out. Whether it was the *Cleopatra* style of over exaggeration – especially in make-up that accentuated enough blue eye shadow to send Maybelline stock soaring – or the young Bohemian look characterized by jumpers, trench coats, turtlenecks, and boots, fashion had lost its focus. And, sadly, much of its grace and beauty, too.

It was the year of Annette Funicello, beach blanket bingo, and, on November 22, an end to the now-famous "Summer of Innocence."

To the shock of a nation, Camelot was over.

 ## Sandra Dee
1·9·6·3

Words fail me!

1·9·6·3

Lena Horne

Sings great, for Lena – shows bony shoulders and reminds one of a plucked chicken. "You can't always look good, Lena, but you could look better."

1·9·6·3
6

Barbra Streisand

All stars have gimmicks, okay! But the tablecloth bit just isn't for stars. Greenwich Village is still a sideshow. Barbra, why reject your obligation to your audience? It's a good thing you didn't set a trend.

NOTES of INTEREST

1963 proved to be a fateful year. For the first – but certainly not last – time, eternal fashion fiascos Elizabeth Taylor and Barbra Streisand joined the worst-dressed ranks – beginning a thirty-year saga of now-mythic design dementia. Barbra and Elizabeth, who co-habit a unique stratosphere of bad taste and schizophrenic style, epitomized the old adage that you can lead a legend to elegant water, but you can't make her drink – or buy a decent dress, for that matter.

Zsa Zsa Gabor, after being named one of the worst dressed three years in a row, enjoyed the rare aura of being the first woman "retired" to the category of Lifetime Member of the Worst Dressed Club. She called me a "naughty, naughty boy," uttered a few unintelligible phrases in Hungarian, doused herself with diamonds, and got married again — not necessarily in that order.

Shirley and Bette were repeat offenders. MacLaine most likely was being paid back for a particularly unsavory past life. And as for Bette, well, I can only guess she preferred good scripts over good style any day of the week. She certainly proved it every time she stepped out of the house. And as she stopped traffic in her garish getups, her phrase "Fasten your seatbelts" suddenly had a whole new meaning.

Ginger Rogers

7

1·9·6·3

When the Castle Walk is revived she'll be back in style.

1·9·6·3

Jill St. John

8

Jill is a beauty, accessories by Woolworths – clothes by Bad Taste.

1·9·6·3

Jayne Meadows

9

Looks like all the stores in town had a sale — and she bought it all; what's worse, she wore it.

1·9·6·3

10

Bette Davis

The great lady of the cinema looks like a dowager queen from Delancey Street.

1964

Worst

19 1 64

Barbra Streisand

A tree grew in Brooklyn – dressed in tablecloth and furs. Claims she has furs for every occasion, but must be getting her occasions mixed. Her high black stockings and shoulder chain purse make one think of an unsuccessful hitchhiker.

> *"You think beautiful girls are gonna stay in style forever?"*
> – 1964 LISTMAKER BARBRA STREISAND, IN *FUNNY GIRL*, LYRIC BY BOB MERRILL
>
> *"It's not your face we're worried about, Barbra."*
> – MR. BLACKWELL

"YOUTH CULTURE" was the operative phrase in categorizing the fashions of 1964. Short and loose, sheer and sexy, were the key to the under-30 infatuation that swept across America. Phrases like "far out," "groovy," and "kooky," became fashion buzz words, and designers emphasized bold blocks of color, sharp outlines, and colored borders. The above-the-knee look was gaining in popularity and colored tights and textured stockings added to the Giacometti-like silhouettes that strode down every city and town in America.

The Beatles brought long, straight hair into vogue for men and women, while Rudi Gernreich introduced the most hideous fashion scam ever perpetrated on the American woman – the "topless", a design which won him the prestigious Coty Award for fashion. The industry, once again in love with nudity for simple shock value, had become a national joke, and I was leading the protest all the way to Seventh Avenue.

Body stockings were introduced to extraordinary success. Transparent sports blouses, evening dresses of sheer lace over nude chiffon, and necklines that dipped down, down, down became the rule not the exception – a rule that was certainly meant to be broken if there ever was one.

In 1964 it became increasingly clear that the fashion industry didn't give two hoots for the average American woman. If you weren't Edie Sedgwick thin, didn't have an endless pocketbook to purchase the carousel of cartoon clothes hanging from every store rack, or were over the age of twenty, you were in trouble. The industry had discovered that the youth culture had lots of money, insecurity, and nerve – the three classic ingredients every major new fad is founded on.

P. T. Barnum once said that there was a sucker born every minute. In 1964, his prophecy was never more accurate – and never more depressing.

1964

 2

Jayne Mansfield

After appearing like a stuffed sausage for many years, Jayne has resorted to the baby pink look – between baby doll shorties and darling pink bows for her multicolored hair, groomed not unlike the sweeping end of a broom. Has she in confusion borrowed her young daughter's wardrobe? Watch out, Mother Mansfield.

1·9·6·4

 3

Debbie Reynolds

A caricature of Zsa Zsa Gabor who is a caricature of . . . well, I really don't know. Plug her in and there's your Christmas tree.

Phyllis Diller

1·9·6·4 **4**

Looks like a scarecrow hung on a clothesline after a heavy windstorm. Designers' mistakes and overturned trash cans have been coordinated to make her the most ridiculously worst-dressed woman.

Cara Williams

1·9·6·4 **5**

TV's most beautiful face! Looks as though she borrowed Salvation Army discards. Total loss of femininity. Should be playing the title role of *Hello Charlie*.

1·9·6·4 **6**

Pamela Mason

Self-admittedly Los Angeles's greatest man hater: bouffant hair, years outdated, bangled sweaters – a look reserved for hand-me-downs, plunging necklines revealing a comically sensuous bustline and too many yards of flesh poured into too few inches of fabric. In sum, a totally confused matron.

1·9·6·4 **7**

Jayne Meadows

May I have an aspirin?

1·9·6·4
⑧ Carol Channing

Painted lips, mascaraed eyes, wearing that bird of paradise. When *Gentlemen Prefer Blondes* is revived, her clothes will be in style again.

1·9·6·4
⑨ Tuesday Weld

Looks as if she just got out of bed and grabbed the top sheet for a gown, but that's Tuesday. Maybe we should see her on Wednesday.

1·9·6·4
⑩
Carroll Baker

It isn't what she does with clothes, it's what she does without them. She's a sexy girl if you like Huckleberry Finn.

NOTES of INTEREST

Vera Jane Palmer – also known as Jayne Mansfield – changed her look for 1964; her pink period was even cheaper in style than her bust-baring past and twice as mind-boggling. She looked like a Pepto Bismol ad without the medicinal benefits. After seeing Jayne parade around Hollywood in her peppermint cloud, Pepto Bismol was, ironically, the perfect antidote.

Barbra Streisand, basking in the Broadway box-office bouquets tossed her way for *Funny Girl*, was entering her nouveau riche period, circa 1964-1972. Hopelessly misguided, and obviously desperate for a singular look to match her singular voice, Barbra – who makes the word *perfectionist* seem sloppy – bombed. With one foot in the couture establishment and one in studied bohemia, Streisand symbolized every square girl across America trying too hard to be hip. Although she kept belting on about "people needing people," I felt what Barbra really needed was an honest designer willing to spend a few years teaching her the fashion ropes. Obviously, no one was.

And then there was Debbie Reynolds, direct from her engagement as America's most put-upon divorcée. Eddie and Liz had done her wrong. So, too, had her mirror if it hadn't cracked right down the middle when faced with those getups!

But for sheer, unadulterated nerve, America's first female standup comic, the ground-breaking Phyllis Diller, caused entire continents of taste to sink into oblivion when she waddled on stage. Looking like Cruella Deville on acid, Phyllis proved the biggest joke of the evening was her wardrobe.

Carol Channing, giving Streisand a run for her money as the worst dressed star on Broadway, wowed the world singing "Before the Parade Passes By" from her hit musical, *Hello Dolly!* She missed it by ten years.

1965

ZEN, GURUS, INDIAN RE-treats, the mystic arts –1965 saw them all. Every social fad, obscure avenue of expression, and unconventional fashion was explored, pontificated over, and dissected by a hungry-for-change population. The revolution of the sixties was hitting its stylized stride, and *tradition* and *elegance* became dirty words. People expressed themselves by rejecting time-worn principles and beliefs; some of the change was good, some was bad. And then there was Courrèges – the fashion designer of the year, who epitomized the magic and the mundane extremes that infiltrated the decade.

Courrèges – from France (where else?) – was a designing genius who had one fatal flaw: no one looked good in his ground-breaking fashions ex-cept flat-chested, anorexic 12-year-olds. Unfortunately since no 12-year-old I know could afford a Courrèges label, much less a "dress," that left a defenseless population at the mercy of a man who saw fashion as a series of asexual uniforms characterized by ultra-short skirts, geometrically con-structed body lines, helmetlike head-gear, huge round goggles, and the obligatory white kid boots to mid-calf. The look was dramatic, future based, shocking, and beyond anyone's wild-est imagination. Hence, the raves began rolling in, and women across America began to re-semble a 1950s science fiction pot-boiler without the happy ending.

The look was wild, way out, win-some, wacky, and white, white, white. Courrèges boots were the only foot-wear of choice. If one did opt for color, subtleties were not allowed. It was a radical either/or situation: either pur-est white or wildest op art psychedelic hues were worn. Nothing in between was allowed. The look was loud, biz-arre, and resembled a Salvador Dali nightmare sprung to life. Little wonder dark glasses became the most impor-tant fashion accessory of the year.

Worst
1 1965

Princess Margaret Rose

A grand revival of *Charlie's Aunt* with a rock'n roll beat.

1·9·6·5 ② Barbra Streisand

Ringo Starr in drag.

Brigitte Bardot 1·9·6·5 ③

It's a good thing no one recognizes her with her clothes on because she dresses like Eve fleeing the Garden of Eden one step ahead of the cops.

> *"When I go outside I'll wear long black boots so that the snakes can't bite me. The world is full of them, you know."*
> – 1965 LISTMAKER MIA FARROW, QUOTED IN KITTY KELLEY'S *HIS WAY*
>
> *"The world is also full of go-go-booted toothpicks with a bad fashion attitude."*
> – MR. BLACKWELL

Mia Farrow

1·9·6·5 **4**

Stretch pants on angel food with hot fudge frosting. She dresses like a 12-year-old and dates Frank Sinatra.

Phyllis Diller

1·9·6·5 **5**

Early disaster. One look at her and birds are ashamed of feathers.

Julie Andrews

1·9·6·5 **6**

Box pleats and old lavender direct from the Montgomery Ward 1940 catalogue.

Madame Charles De Gaulle

1·9·6·5 **7**

Behind every successful man there is a woman, and this one is about twenty years behind.

My seemingly life-long fashion battle with the British royal family began in 1965, when I put Princess Margaret at the top of the list. Personally, I have always found Margaret to be one of the most fascinating of the staid monarchy. Her passionate 1950s love affair with Captain Peter Townshend ended in bittersweet denial; Margaret – a victim of senseless Victorian morality – was not allowed to marry the love of her life because – Ye Gads! – Captain Townsend was divorced. Instead she married Lord Snowdon in 1960 and began a whirlwind life-style that found her at every chic discotheque, avant-garde party, and hip nightclub across the globe. Ironically, Margaret's marriage to Lord Snowdon ended in divorce in 1976. But by then divorce was no longer a blasphemous condition of the heart.

In 1965, Margaret was the royal joke: spoiled, capricious, headstrong, and beautiful. She dressed like the tarts along London's trendiest avenue, Carnaby Street, and managed to embarrass not only her family but herself as well. She danced with the Beatles and Richard Burton and Elizabeth Taylor. She threw royal caution to the wind, and most probably enjoyed causing her older sister a few headaches since their showdown over Peter Townshend years before. I wasn't about to get involved in any family arguments, but I did think that Margaret was a disaster and I said so. The press reaction in England was explosive, to say the least. You'd have thought I pulled off the Queen Mother's wig in public. I was labeled a blasphemous American upstart – and have never lived it down.

Julie Andrews – America's favorite British nanny, Mary Poppins – had also been embroiled in a little controversy of her own in 1965. Word got out she swore like a sailor and was hardly the equivalent of her latest screen incarnation, Maria Von Trapp in *The Sound of Music*, which put her on a prim and proper pedestal that, in retrospect, hurt her more than it helped. Her clothes were as sugary sweet as her PR image and disguised a vibrant, outspoken, talented woman.

On an even heavier note, 1965 saw the Battle of the Bulge begin for Elizabeth Taylor, a battle that must be one of the longest and most meticulously chronicled in modern times. So much for consciousness-raising – what everyone really wanted to know was how much Liz weighed.

1·9·6·5

8

Lucille Ball

Halloween trick without the treat. Lucy, dear, shoulder pads went out with the black bottom.

1·9·6·5

9

Bette Davis

Whatever happened to Baby Jane? She became Tallulah Bankhead cast as Marshal Dillon.

1·9·6·5

10

Elizabeth Taylor

In tight sweaters and skirts she looks like a chain of link sausages.

1966

THE YEAR OF THE miniskirt had arrived in a major way. The youth craze had reached its body-conscious zenith in 1966. Aged dowagers who had never dreamed of wearing a dress at knee length now turned to shorter styles. It was not a particularly thrilling sight. In fact, the mini moment was lost on nearly everyone except *Vogue* models and those very few who really did have great legs. The vast majority, pre-Jane Fonda Workout days, managed to re-semble nothing more than plump, plucked chickens in a paisley covered barnyard.

The ultra-short lengths gave unprecedented significance to the leg. The knobby knee became the new "erogenous zone," to the detriment of the bust, hip, and waist, which were understated by designers to the point of oblivion. Stockings and leotards completed the Tinkertoy ambience that stalked society in 1966.

Accessories were typified by ugly, wide leather belts that might have looked good on Matt Dillon but no one else. Waist lines drop-ped to the hipbone, which meant that women wore their tie-dyed jeans three inches lower than usual, causing embarrassing stom-ach bulges to magically appear. The "Dunlap" look (done lapped over your belt) was almost as bad as its fashion opposite, the irre-pressible mini. If there ever was a case when two wrongs don't make a right, these two omnipresent

1966 styles were it.

London's Carnaby Street – and its pale, pink, glacially mod mascot, model Jean Shrimpton – introduced all kinds of creative, outrageous, unwearable clothes. Plastic jumpers, coats, and dresses were haute chic – and haute hideous. The wild patterns and op art prints so popular in 1965 were yesterday's news; fashion was throwaway, immediate, as ever-changing as Elizabeth Taylor's figure (especially after *Who's Afraid of Virginia Woolf*, which dumbfounded a nation).

And then there was the appear-ance of the paper dress – *the* perfect symbol of the vapidity that epitomized the year in fashion. The paper dress lasted as long on the woman as the fad itself: about an hour.

Worst
19 · 1 · 66
Mia Farrow

A Girl Scout cookie in a martini at Arthur's.

1·9·6·6
2 Julie Andrews

A plain-Jane Pollyanna playing Peter Pan at half-mast.

1·9·6·6
3 Elizabeth Taylor

A boutique toothpaste tube, squeezed from the middle.

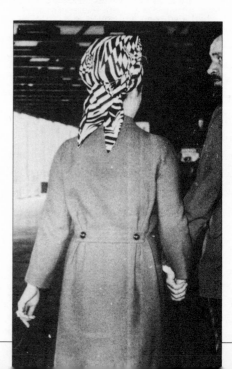

1·9·6·6
4

Ann-Margret

Marlon Brando in a G-string.

5

Carol Channing

Finger paints, chicken feathers, and glue thrown into an electric fan.

1·9·6·6

6

Maria Callas

No Italian would have ever paid for those dresses! Beware of Greeks bearing gifts.

1·9·6·6

7

Governor Lurleen Wallace
(of Alabama)

Next Monday's wash in a broken washing machine.

Liza Minnelli

8 1·9·6·6

Pop-art picture of a fried egg at sunrise, eaten by Auntie Em.

Simone Signoret

9 1·9·6·6

The Eiffel Tower without the Paris influence.

> *"I'm me. I've made it on my own."*
> – 1966 LISTMAKER LIZA MINNELLI
>
> *"You certainly did, Liza, in more ways than one."*
> – MR. BLACKWELL

NOTES of INTEREST

It seemed tradition was only kept alive by the appearance of past fashion disasters Mia, Julie, Elizabeth, and Carol. Everywhere else – from movies to politics – progress in spite of everything was the feeling throughout the land. But some things never change, and the coterie of women that appeared on the list year in and year out was somehow comforting. As a matter of fact, the sheer inevitability that Mia Farrow, the new Mrs. Frank Sinatra, would appear looking like a Technicolor scarecrow guaranteed a laugh. But not as long as Frank was around, if you know what I mean.

Opera diva Maria Callas – she of extraordinary voice, passion, and mistress to Aristotle Onassis fame – should have stuck to singing. Her gowns were a symphony of wrong notes, bad chords, and lousy executions; her designer should have been executed instead. But Maria remained impossibly enigmatic, even if she did look like the Athenian ruins at twilight.

Not so Milton Berle – the first man so accorded the "honor" of appearing on the Worst Dressed List. Berle, because of his petrifying penchant for dressing in drag at every available chance on television, was dutifully honored. But the Callas charisma was sadly lacking in this bag of beaded bones. Berle's knobby knees alone could have stopped a shortchanged New York cab driver at fifty paces. In other words, Milton was a must for the list. Anyone who can do that deserves all the attention he can get.

I made fellow Alabaman Jim Nabors so mad when I put his Governor, Lurleen Wallace, on the list that he demanded an apology on national television one night when I was appearing on "The Joey Bishop Show." Of course, I refused, but Gomer Pyle was not to be denied. Things got sticky but I held my ground – but never my tongue. Certain things are sacred.

Truman Capote's legendary Black and White Ball at the Plaza gave me momentary hope that fashion wasn't dead, just comatose. Even Mia Farrow Sinatra managed to look relatively decent in a white beaded sheath on that most glittering of nights. And that – not *In Cold Blood* – might have been Tru's most unbelievable achievement. I love the story Gerald Clarke tells about the extravagance of that evening: Gloria Guinness was forced to stay in bed the following day due to exhaustion – wearing too many pounds of diamonds and rubies around her swanlike neck had simply worn her to a frazzle. Who said glamour was dead? At least someone had the right idea.

And then there was newcomer Liza Minnelli, who must have received her fashion sense from a friend of the family: the Wicked Witch of the West.

1·9·6·6

⑩

Milton Berle

With padded brassiere and corseted rear, the her that appears really isn't!

1967

FLOWER POWER WAS IN full, fragrant bloom. If the clothes associated with the love and peace movement of the mid-sixties were less than flattering to the average woman – or man – at least the message of the movement was, to me, wonderfully refreshing. The Beatles recorded "All You Need is Love" on a sunny, June 14 afternoon in 1967, and with that anthem, the psychedelic era in fashion, music, art, and film burst into worldwide view. Soon, "Sgt. Pepper" would dominate society in a way no one imagined popular music ever could.

And since fashion is one of the single most important barometers of a society, 1967 showed us that a revolution was happening right before our granny-glassed eyes. Vietnam was no longer acceptable. The status quo was no longer sought. The establishment was suddenly a blasphemous group of warmongers.

Social and political rules were made to be smashed. Fashion was the frenetic reaction to the U-turn toward individuality, creativity, and civil freedom. Too bad most of it turned out to be another kind of mass uniform, worn as religiously as the pin-stripes of the Brooks Brothers brigade on Wall Street.

Love beads. Bell bottoms. T-shirts. Silk brocade jackets. Torn blue jeans. Miniskirts. Above-the-knee boots. Antique brooches. Leather vests. It was an eclectic, color-drenched hodge-podge of cheap glittered, Patchouli-aroma'd, bizarrely designed duds, which managed to resemble an endless carnival roaming the cities and towns of America. But this time there was no exit to the parking lot. What you saw was what you got, and most of the time the vision was Hitchcockian at best.

The "hippie" label meant iconoclastic, strident, and unconventional taken to new peaks of fashion faddism. Still, like a stalwart soldier standing in the rain, the "little black dress" somehow made a comeback in 1967, perhaps because people were color-blind by this point and needed a respite from the rainbows darting and dashing everywhere. Other big news in couture centered on Yves St. Laurent's trouser suits in black velvet for evening. Pants for evening? You bet. The world did – and lost. Courreges returned with the one-piece jumpsuit while a to-the-floor length skirt called the "maxi" entered the fashion sweepstakes. The only loser was the confused consumer.

"Laughter is much more important than applause."
– LISTMAKER CAROL CHANNING

"And the punchline – to anyone with two eyes and courage enough to look – was La Channing herself, whose outfits had 'em rolling in the aisles, on the streets, and beyond."
– MR. BLACKWELL

1967

③

Jayne Meadows

A Barnum & Bailey circus in a telephone booth.

1·9·6·7

④

Elizabeth Taylor

Looks like two small boys fighting under a mink blanket.

1·9·6·7

⑤

Julie Andrews

A rejected cover girl for a Charles Dickens novel.

1·9·6·7

⑥

Carol Channing

The blonde bombshell who looks like George Sand caught in a wind tunnel.

1967

1·9·6·7
7

Raquel Welch

A Dresden reproduction of Charles Atlas wearing Band-Aids.

1·9·6·7
8

Ann-Margret

A Hell's Angels escapee that invaded the Ziegfeld Follies on a rainy night.

Vanessa Redgrave

A do-it-yourself kit on stilts that came unglued.

1·9·6·7
10

1·9·6·7
9

Jane Fonda

Stretch pants on angel food cake.

Good Grief!

On April 18, 1966, Julie Christie shocked the usually staid Academy Awards when she accepted her Best Actress Oscar for *Darling* in gold micro-mini pajamas "designed" by Don Bessant, revealing much more skin than style. Still, I resisted putting her on the list in 1966 mainly because the ten that made it were infinitely worse than even Miss Christie. But all that changed in 1967, when I could no longer deny the series of mini skirted disasters Julie paraded around in. Even by Hollywood standards she was too much, too soon, and, although she and I were quite fond of one another, Julie placed number two. I thought Julie was too talented to reduce herself to the fairground exhibitionist level and told her so. Her tea boiled on its own.

Liz, Barbra, Julie A., and Carol, that quartet of quintessential couture quacks, were still included. Believe me, if there had been a way to exclude them, I would've. But a bad fashion accident is unavoidable, and these walking wrecks screamed out for attention. And they got it, in spades.

The selection of Raquel Welch began a multi-year run of body-baring bombs that brought back memories of Jayne Mansfield on a particularly petrifying day. "Racky," as her friends were known to call her, was just plain "tacky," devoid of the kind of charisma her predecessors – Mae, Marilyn, Rita, and Ava – possessed. As Andy Warhol once noted, Raquel was the only big star he could think of who never appeared in a hit movie. If that's the case, her fashion sense was big-time bomb quality, too.

A very unliberated Jane Fonda hit the top ten in 1967 – she of tight sweaters, tight pants, and tight tummy. Jane was still searching for an image during the mid-sixties. The one she inhabited in 1967 was more "Kitten with a Whip" than "Crusader with a Cause." Vanessa Redgrave's on-screen nudity was more political in nature: *Blowup* was the sensation of the year. Unlike Fonda, Vanessa had already discovered her social consciousness, claiming, "I'm about as left wing as it's possible to go." Her fashions were more southbound – straight to hell, to be precise.

And then there was Ann-Margret. Like Jane Fonda in *Barbarella*, Ann-Margret had yet to discover the unique gifts she so decorously hid behind a wall of cleavage and pursed lips. Their time would come – and not a moment too soon.

1968

THE UBIQUITOUS PANT-suit overshadowed the mini in 1968, not a particularly difficult chore considering the material involved. Or lack thereof. Nevertheless, the "Sun King" himself, YSL, revolutionized the fashion industry with the sudden – yes, even arrogant – switch to pants in 1967. In 1968 the look swept across the nation like wildfire, mercifully covering up the bumps and bulges the mini so callously exposed. I suppose the pantsuit was the lesser of two egregious evils: on most women the "trouser suit," as the fashion industry called it, made a dowdy, dumpy, and dull statement. But women were ready to cover up again and YSL, a clever and, yes, visionary, businessman, knew the mini couldn't last. And he was right. And besides, designers could charge twice as much for a pantsuit as a mini, which utilized lots of shapeless material and lots of bad taste. The only dissenters, besides myself, were a few snooty restaurants who refused to allow women to wear pants during the dinner hour. That tempest in a teapot lasted until the restaurateurs began losing their starched shirts in revenues and gave in – like all the rest.

The maxi look sputtered fitfully, grew dim, and died a quick, unheralded death. But the real losers were the consumers who wasted the family savings on a look that lasted as long as Tiny Tim tiptoeing through the tulips.

In addition to the pantsuit par-

ade, which in itself was distressing enough, an entire galaxy of accessories were created to accompany YSL's brainchild. Braided and jeweled waistcoats, wide belts, and ruffled shirts were de rigueur. The creepy combination of pants and frilly blouses made most women look like the local circus trainer auditioning for Barnum & Bailey's.

In the fall, helmets, hoods, and the occasional turban hid the face as best they could. But the real hair style – as seen on soul legend Aretha Franklin – was the Afro. Her hair was as big as her voice, but on an army of others, shock therapy side effect was the immediate reaction when running into those electrocuted curls rigid in the wind.

The Queen of Fashion, Jackie K, became Jackie O in October, and segued, fashionwise, into her own Greek tragedy.

Julie Andrews

A Little Bo-Peep illustration for *True Love* magazine.

1·9·6·8

Carol Burnett

Looks like a tornado hit the bargain basement and Carol collected it all.

 ③
1·9·6·8

The Lennon Sisters

Should be called the "Lemon Sisters," because their wardrobe hits a sour note. Someone should tell these young matrons they aren't vintage 1945 June Allysons.

Vanessa Redgrave

 1·9·6·8
⑤

The rocket to stardom that launched Vanessa to success missed its target when she got dressed.

Kaye Ballard

1·9·6·8
 ④

Prince Valiant in a panty girdle.

Mr. Blackwell's Worst: Thirty Years of Fashion Fiascos

1968

1·9·6·8

6

Doris Day

Has she stayed too long
at the fair?

1·9·6·8

7

Raquel Welch

She may have a heavenly body but her
clothes look like they were designed by the
Man in the Moon – a real luna-tic.

1·9·6·8

8

Mama Cass

Little Orphan Annie in gowns by
Oscar Meyer.

1·9·6·8

9

*Brigitte
Bardot*

Needs an architect instead
of a designer. Brigitte's a real
space odyssey – or is it a
space oddity? We wish she
would just go on her own
Milky Way.

1·9·6·8

10

Jane Fonda

A real grown-up Barbie
doll. Aspirin, please.

After years of swimming in the mid-range of the list, Julie Andrews finally sank all the way to number one in 1968. Her homespun look made Shirley Temple seem positively pornographic by comparison. Julie, taking her *Sound of Music* image to the height of saccharine-sweet virginity, was so retro, especially in 1968, that she defied originality at every timid turn.

I heard through the grapevine that Carol Burnett wasn't at all pleased with my back-handed tribute, but after the garish getups she thrust our way, I suspected she had more in common with that other carrot-topped clown, Lucille Ball, than just a great way with a line. Both women were hymns to hilarity, and in 1968, so, too, were their fashions. But Carol's were the worst: a tragedy of comedic proportions only the Marx Brothers could appreciate.

The Lennon Sisters, like a quartet of Julie Andrews clones (without the Marine haircut Julie refused to relinquish), were the antithesis of fashion progress and the epitome of yesterday's mistakes in the clothes department. All those Lawrence Welk champagne bubbles must have gone to their over-coiffed heads.

Larger-than-life folksinger Mama Cass, heading for a breakup with The Mamas and the Papas, was a recipe for overabundant nerve, empty couture calories, and too much "California Dreaming" under the sun, causing an eclipse, fashionwise.

Raquel, Jane, and Vanessa were back for the second time, while Doris Day, as effervescent as ever, fizzed out when it came to developing a modern, sophisticated style. For Doris, who seemed unable to reach beyond her *Pillow Talk* fetish for pink, pink, pink, made me see red, red, red. "Que Sera Sera" indeed.

> *"No one else will ever be Bardot. I am the only Bardot, and my species is unique."*
> – 1968 LISTMAKER BRIGITTE BARDOT
>
> *"She does have a point – or two."*
> – MR. BLACKWELL

Brigitte Bardot – who had, in spite of her bad taste, developed a real style for herself – appeared in the Westernized *Shalako* portraying Countess Irina Lazaar – a role as unbelievable as Bardot's negligible wardrobe off screen. Her barely there ensembles were as muddled as her English and twice as wispy.

Queen
Elizabeth II

Everything that is out of
fashion is in with the Queen –
Hail, Victoria!

T HE FACT THAT TINY
Tim and Miss Vickie's
televised marriage on the
Johnny Carson Show drew the
largest late-night audience ever
gave one an indication how low we
had sunk, and fashions were right
behind.

What a year! The pantsuit was
still hanging around, like a virus
no one could shake. Older women
began to complain – loudly – to
retailers that there was nothing
for them to buy. The retailers,
however, were in a *Catch-22*
situation. You can't sell something
that's unavailable, and designers
simply had forgotten anyone over
30 and over size 8.

It was the Woodstock summer
– August, to be exact. The topless
troops that infiltrated the tiny
New York town threw fashion –
and caution – out the window. A
sea of bell-bottomed, flower-
decked, Medusa-haired children
let the sunshine in – and escorted
good taste out.

Fashion, more than ever,
revolved around the stars of
music, not cinema. The Beatles
still influenced, but the real
trendsetters were Jim Morrison
and his tight leather pants, Mick
Jagger's unisex blending of hyper
masculinity and model-slim
femininity, and Janis Joplin's mix
of jeans, granny glasses, and
feather boas, all loaded down
with more cheap jewelry than the
nation's combined five-and-

dime's. It was a sight for someone
else's eyes; a mere glimpse gave
me a psyche-delic migraine. I
didn't need Jimi Hendrix's guitar
to electrify my senses; his clothes
did it for me.

In less wacky waters, fashion
still drowned. The long, flat,
clinging look was unflattering at
best; tops grew longer while skirts
remained ultra-short for
those who chose to wear
them.

The tunic was re-
introduced, shown with
flaring pants or brief
flared skirt. Sleeveless
jumpers worn over
contrasting long-sleeved
shirts were popular with
the space-suit crowd.
Shoes were chunky,
giving women the effect
of walking on colored
tree stumps. Where are termites
when you need them?

I said a fond adieu to the
insufferable sixties and
uttered a silent prayer
for the seventies. I knew
we were going to need it,
but even I had
no idea how truly
tacky the next
decade would be.

> *"I'm afraid there are rather
> a lot of dogs."*
> – 1969 LISTMAKER QUEEN
> ELIZABETH II, TO A GUEST
> VISITING THE MONARCH AT
> SANDRINGHAM, HER COUNTRY
> RETREAT, IN ROBERT LACEY'S
> *MAJESTY.*
>
> *"Was she referring to her
> corgis or her clothes? Only
> her lady-in-waiting knows for
> sure."*
> – MR. BLACKWELL

1·9·6·9

②

Barbra Streisand

Yesterday's see-through . . .
chemise, schlemiel, and 23 Skiddoo,
and what happened to you?

1·9·6·9

③ ## Raquel Welch

From Welch – you could belch!

1·9·6·9

④

Jacqueline Susann

Tillie the Toiler gone
bad in the Valley of the
Falls – hair, that is!

1969

5

Goldie Hawn

A peeled grape on the end of a pipe cleaner! Has the fickle finger of fashion passed her by?

1·9·6·9

Carol Burnett

Looks like the last float in last year's Rose Parade. Or, a Grandma Moses' painting of a petunia patch. Tacky, Tacky, Tacky, Tacky!

1·9·6·9

7

Doris Day

Doing your own thing in blushing pink . . . but for thirty years?

1·9·6·9

8

Shirley Temple

The dimpled darling of the "Good Ship Lollipop" wearing "Disjointed Notions"!

1·9·6·9

9

Mae West

High camp exploding in a bon-bon factory!

1·9·6·9

10

Ann-Margret

Moisten lips . . . hair in flips . . . boots and sequins . . . what a miss?

The worst outfit of 1969, perhaps even the decade, and the absolute nadir of any gown ever worn to the Academy Awards, was Barbra Joan Streisand's now-legendary transparent pajama nightmare by Scaasi, which she donned to pick up her Best Actress trophy for *Funny Girl*. On this momentous evening, Barbra was more tragic than amusing, causing Oscar-cast fashion consultant Edith Head's black glasses to emit more steam than a Chinese laundry. No one could have guessed, as a seated Streisand demurely glanced toward her soon-to-be-ex, Elliot Gould, as the nominations were read, just how grotesque her "gown" really was. All the at-home viewer could see was a very prim and proper black bow, starched white collar, and cuffs. From the bustline up she looked like a nun. Below resembled an entirely different occupation. When Streisand's name was announced by Ingrid Bergman as the co-winner (she tied with Katharine Hepburn for *The Lion In Winter*), and as she made her way to the stage, the grins became gasps . . . and a galaxy of groans. Barbra was wearing, or not wearing, a glittery, see-through pantsuit with balloon legs and sleeves, under which black panties and bra were more than merely apparent. To make a bad situation worse, she tripped climbing the steps to the podium and the world was treated to a disconcerting close-up of Streisand's nearly nude derrière. (From the way the Academy ignored Barbra in the ensuing years, her "mooning" of the membership was, perhaps, a bit of poetic justice.) Striding toward an open-mouthed Ingrid Bergman, Streisand seemed oblivious to the fact that her getup was one of the great mistakes in fashion history; she hit a new low note in a wardrobe that was chock full of musical discord. Barbra's out-of-place illusion caused a rash of see-through disasters to hit the streets in a homage of horror to the styleless songbird.

At least Barbra was young and impressionable. What was Queen Elizabeth's excuse? Her uniform of utilitarian ugliness was beyond bad; it was dreadfully boring in the best British tradition. The matching hats, coats, dresses, handbags, and shoes were beyond out – they were positively prehistoric. Queen Elizabeth II looked more like a dowdy Sunday school teacher than ruler of an Empire. But the loyal Londoners stood by their relic of a regent, and tossed a lot more than crumpets my way. With visions of the Tower of London in my mind, I avoided merry ol' England for the next few years – either that or become the first American designer to grace Madame Tussaud's torture chamber.

When Truman Capote called Jackie Susann a "truck driver in drag," she threatened to sue – until she realized all Capote would have to do to convince a jury of the accuracy of his attack would be to parade a few truck drivers in drag through the courtroom. No jury in the world would convict "the tiny terror" of slander when confronted with the evidence.

The

S E V E N T I E S

Worst
19 1 70

Sophia loren

A 1950 B movie costumed by
Polly Adler!

1·9·7·0
2

Angie
Dickinson

Venus covered in fish net!

1·9·7·0
3

Gloria
Vanderbilt
Cooper

Jet-set's funny folly.
The all-American Gypsy!

1·9·7·0 **4**

Shelley
Winters

The skinny dip look
on a stuffed sausage.

1·9·7·0 **5**

Jacqueline
Susann

A fright wig on a closed
umbrella!

1·9·7·0 **6**

Carrie
Snodgress

Wardrobe by early
attic and late basement!

1970

NOT A MOMENT TO catch our breath as the decade began, or to attempt to understand the crazy circus of styles, color, and fabric that had characterized the sixties, because word from high whispered that what had come before was merely couture under the bridge as far as 1970 was concerned.

John Fairchild, the single-minded leader of *Women's Wear Daily*, the fashion bible for global fashion-addicts everywhere, decreed that "the longuette" – or the midi, in less pretentious terms – was the look of the new decade. Gone were the flower-power embroidered jeans, the gold lamé microminis, the cluttered, junky, funky synergy of the sixties. When Fairfhild decided that the image of the sixties was dead, I heartily agreed. But what Fairchild so arrogantly proposed to replace the mini moment with was just as God-awful, if not, God forbid, worse.

The midi revolution caught everyone by mid-calfed surprise: the buyers moaned, the stores groaned, and the consumers wandered about the racks of granny-length dresses in shock. Sheer ugliness had never been as mundane – or as expensive. The yo-yo skirt length syndrome had initially intrigued – even excited – the fashionable ladies of the sixties, but now, after too many boomerangs from the sanctimonious sanctuary of Seventh Avenue,

women across America were just plain mad. And broke. The midi meant an entirely new wardrobe, from shoes to blouses to accessories. For the first time, the public told John Fairchild just where he could put his latest brainstorm – and it most certainly wasn't in an area he could openly discuss over lunch at Le Cirque.

Still, the disciples at the *WWD* shrine kept the midi in the news much longer than it had any right to be, while such accessories as shoulder bags, flowing scarfs à la Isadora Duncan, wide belts, and garish jewelry completed the turgid look.

The pantsuit was, unfortunately, still popular with the K-Mart crowd and jersey, in all its non-natural stretch appeal, was the fabric of choice. Young girls adopted the straight-haired, parted down the middle coiffure popularized by Ali MacGraw in *Love Story* – a look as limp as her acting ability.

And so, the decade began with a whimper, not a bang – and such future trends as hot pants, no-bust couture, trash/flash, and disco waited in the wings like a costly cobra, ready to strike.

7

Jane Fonda

A *Tobacco Road*
escapee on a
motorcycle.

8
1·9·7·0

Goldie Hawn

A shaggy dog on stilts . . . wearing
Band-Aids!

1·9·7·0

9

Marlo Thomas

Halloween
every day!

46

The midi length was popularized by two actresses on the 1970 list, Carrie *"Diary of a Mad Housewife"* Snodgress and Jane "Welcome to the Revolution" Fonda. Snodgress, who had won critical raves for her role as a depressed housewife in Frank Perry's drama, seemed to take the role home with her, especially in the fashion department. Carrie was just plain scary in her Marin County monstrosities, and seemed to take delight in wearing the dowdiest dresses since Ma Kettle. Jane, who had come into her own as a serious actress with *They Shoot Horses, Don't They?*, obviously decided her sixties bimbo image had hit a social snag. Jane preferred dark, sexless coverups as the seventies sprang into view, replete with shaggy sheepdog hair, no makeup, and a plethora of pants, pants, pants. Barbarella might have been buried with the spandex bras, but Godzilla with the raised fist was as visible as her newfound acting ability.

1969's Best Supporting Actress Oscar winner, Goldie Hawn, had wowed America with her Judy Holliday-like kooky gamin number, not to mention her bikini-clad scene stealers on Rowan and Martin's "Laugh In." Pretty, perky, and promising, Goldie was a very clever girl when it came to her career. When it came to fashion, she delved – with equal success – into epic tragedy. Goldie looked like a prepubescent sunflower trying to be an overlush orchid; her clothes had more curves than she did.

Faye Dunaway was likened to the great stars of the forties – theatrical, strikingly beautiful, sensually elegant. After *The Thomas Crown Affair* no one would look at a chess set in quite the same way. As far as her personal wardrobe was concerned, good taste had been checkmated in favor of a mix-and-match approach that would have stopped Bonnie and Clyde dead in their trigger-happy tracks.

Shelley Winters continued to amaze, but the year's biggest surprise was the usually elegant Sophia Loren, who, since her 1961 inclusion on the list, had begun dressing like the great star she was. In 1970, she – like her movie *Sunflower* – hit a new fashion low. Sophia looked like a Vegas lounge act, even if the jewelry *was* real.

Faye Dunaway

10

1·9·7·0

Mulligan stew. Has Faye done-away with fashion forever?

1971

Pocahontas wearing remnants from Custer's Last Stand!

THE GREATEST FORCE in fashion was gone. Gabrielle (Coco) Chanel died January 10, 1971. One could only imagine her reaction to the latest fad from Seventh Avenue: hot pants.

Since John Fairchild's midi revolution had turned into his own version of Waterloo, the industry clamored for a new statement. Like mad alchemists they combined the mini and the pantsuit and presto: hot pants! Something didn't quite gel in the experiment, to put it as politely as possible. In other words, hot pants stank, taking feminine fashion to new depths of cartoon-like camp.

The uniform evolved into hot pants half concealed under a shaggy mid-length fur coat covering the tops of high boots. One didn't need those stimulants so closely associated with the sixties anymore; one glimpse of this current catastrophe was enough to send someone on a trip to the outer limits forever. If hot pants alone weren't reason enough to question the sanity of the human race, the use of sheer tights, in black or brown, as the appointed accessory, was. The "ensemble" made the midi seem like the good old days.

The sleeveless, deep armholed, deep necked T-shirt became another dubious rage in 1971. Looking more like convicts on parole than women on parade, the cotton swab tops were combined with blue-jeaned bottoms in heretofore unprecedented numbers. No style, no taste, no figure in sight, especially after the layered look took hold in the fall. Six years before Diane Keaton would recapture the bag lady look,

the layered loonies covered up as obsessively as the hot pants devotees threw thigh to the wind.

Battle fatigues, work clothes, Army jackets followed. Chinese work uniforms in blue silk were popular with the Mao movers and shakers. Ghastly, at best.

Jacqueline Onassis

2 1·9·7·1

Kitty of the cat pack . . .
in tom pants!

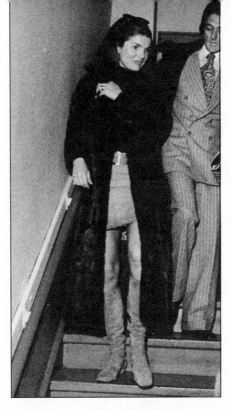

3 1·9·7·1

Princess Anne

The DDT award . . .
dull, dowdy, and tacky!

4 1·9·7·1

Dinah Shore

The belle of the
quilting party looking
like Mary, Mary on a
teeter-totter!

*"What does she do with all
these clothes? I never see her
in anything but blue jeans!"*
– ARISTOTLE ONASSIS ON
JACKIE , FROM *ARI*, BY
PETER EVANS

*"You took the words right out
of my press release."*
– MR. BLACKWELL

1971

5

Jacqueline Susann

Writes love, speaks love . . .
looks like a divorce?

6

1·9·7·1

Carol Burnett

Mass confusion
purchased from a Park
Avenue garage sale!

1·9·7·1

7

Brigitte Bardot

The Betty Boop of
the bosom dolls!

Martha Mitchell

1·9·7·1

8

Sun Bonnet Sue on a
rainy afternoon wearing
chiffon and old lace
twenty years too late!

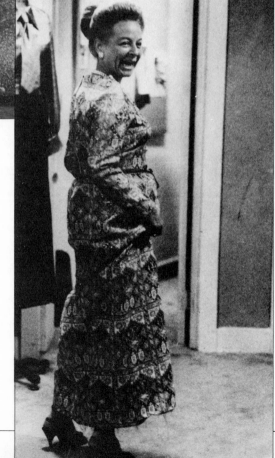

She wears anything she can get her hands on and it shows.

1·9·7·1

10

Twiggy

In a strapless gown, she could sue her bust for nonsupport!

The striking Ali MacGraw struck out in 1971, topping the list for the first time. Beautiful Ali, crooked teeth and all, took prairie chic to the southwestern limit in her pseudo-Indian fringe, scuffed boots, teepee tresses, and feathered silver jewelry. She was ready for the next stagecoach west, but since there were no stagecoaches in Beverly Hills in 1971, she looked a bit out of place – a hundred years to be specific.

Princess Anne joined her mother and aunt in the endless royal fashion fiasco that was quickly establishing itself as yet another questionable British tradition. Anne, with features only a mother (and equestrian) could love, hit the fashion hurdle with a deafening thud – and the grim fact that she smiled about as often as Garbo tap danced nude on 5th Avenue during rush-hour traffic only made her appearances more sinister, with or without the Hanging Gardens of Babylon hats she terrorized her subjects with on a daily basis.

Mrs. Martha Mitchell, wife of Attorney General John Mitchell, was setting the stuffy, hypocritical Capitol Hill crowd on its wiretapped ears. The mouth of the South was as huge as President Nixon's ego, and twice as outspoken. Her fashion sense screamed out, too – for help! Martha had never gotten past the parasol and pastel print syndrome; she resembled a latter-day Scarlett O'Hara after one too many trips to Tara. Still, you couldn't help but love her. She said what she thought, before she thought it.

As silent as Martha was loud, former First Lady Jacqueline Kennedy Onassis had retreated to Skorpios, where she adopted a new look: T-shirts and jeans. Or, on special occasions, the obligatory pantsuit. Why Jackie, of all people, sauntered down the road to fashion ruin was a mystery, but the evidence was frightfully clear, and her no-bra look, which would come into full bloom later, showed too little too late. Like an underdressed schoolboy, Jackie's wardrobe was unisex without the sex – a flat, dreary flop.

And then there was British modeling sensation Twiggy. The only aspect of her persona that worked was her name, which perfectly described the bony branches and barren twigs that erupted from her unfashionable feet. She made Jackie O look like Mae West.

Raquel Welch

But, how do you dress a Sherman Tank?

2

Julie Andrews

She dresses like the kind of woman every man wants for his . . . maiden uncle!

3

Mia Farrow

Around the world in eighty mistakes!

4

Princess Margaret

The kind of styles that make Londoners grateful for their fog!

> *"This success thing is a little scary."*
> – 1972 LISTMAKER ALI MCGRAW
>
> *"Not to mention that horror fest of a wardrobe "*
> – MR. BLACKWELL

19

IT WAS THE YEAR OF THE sweater. Literally millions of sheered sheep roamed the hills and valleys across the states – the baggier the better (or worse, depending on one's viewpoint). Torsos were covered up, disguised, draped, bundled, and wrapped, while below, skin-tight pants emphasizing a racetrack of curves were favored. The overall effect was rather like an A-frame house on stilts teetering toward certain fashion oblivion.

For the more adventurous, the *Cabaret* influence dictated lots of garter belts, red lips, green fingernails, and spidery, grotesque fake eyelashes. As Sally Bowles, Liza Minnelli was brilliant, but as a fashion statement she was beyond bad; decadent disaster was infinitely more accurate. Still, the trendsetters swept through the nightclubs like brazen Berlin babes in need of a very strict curfew – or better yet, a nunnery.

The majority of fashion-conscious women chose comfort over couture, simplicity over sequins. The short flared-back coat worn over trousers was as popular as the nautical look, which was so omnipresent in its

Ali MacGraw

Packs all the glamour of an old worn-out sneaker!

'72

ocean of navy and white I was seasick. The separate jacket paired with low, pleated, print dresses brought the schoolgirl-on-a-picnic image into vogue – and left me out in the cold.

The layered look continued to mix and match itself into a fashion frenzy. The dial-an-outfit syndrome, which enabled women to turn four or five separates into an amazing avalanche of looks, too often got a wrong number. Craftsmanship and originality were out. Excess, at any cost, was in. In the evening hours, strapless tops, plunging necklines, and bare backs with halter necklines deci-mated the morning and afternoon coverups, taking formality to the level of an evening at the ball game – with a strikeout at every turn.

Clogs clogged on. Heels rose to nearly five inches, as thick as building blocks. Young girls who had embraced the mini several years before did an about-face and donned smocks, turtlenecks, and, as was the rule, sweaters for days. From one mistake to another, 1972 was a banner year. Too bad the banner was made of polyester and had no visible means of support.

Lauren Bacall

The epitome of drab. If you want her, just yawn.

1972

Yoko Ono ▷**7** 1·9·7·2

A disaster area in stereo.
Oh no, Yoko!

1·9·7·2 **8** ▽ *Cloris Leachman*

Whether in sportswear or
dresses she always seems to
lack one simple accessory – a
thrift-mart shopping bag!

1·9·7·2 **9** *Alexis Smith*

Her clothes have all the sex appeal of
Henry Kissinger in an unemployment line!

Raquel Welch bobbed into first place with as much gusto and verve as her closest past competitors – Barbra, Julie, and Elizabeth. But whereas the trio of tastelessness had a career to fall back on in 1972, Raquel's clothes – or lack thereof – were her career. What she did on screen certainly couldn't be called acting – more like a lumpy fashion show without the fashion. But, heaven knows, the lumps were shown off to splendid results in such films as *One Million Years B.C.* and *Myra Breckinridge*. I'll never forget the George Eells story about Raquel and her *Myra Breckinridge* co-star, the legendary and at times brutally direct Mae West. Perhaps because Raquel didn't have a clue what sex appeal *really* was – an emotion Mae practically defined – or because Mae was jealous of Raquel's undeniably goddesslike beauty (however vacuous), Welch and West did not see bust to bust on anything. When, during their last scene together, Raquel showed up wearing a red dress with accompanying snood, Mae remarked "These days you can't tell who's the wolf and who's Little Red Riding Hood." Since Mae and Raquel have been targets of mine, I'm sure both would have agreed I could have starred as the wolf any day, if the part hadn't already been filled by Miss Welch herself – in Mae's words, not mine!

The dragon lady of the late sixties and seventies – at least according to the monsoon of publicity surrounding Japanese avant-garde artist Yoko Ono and how she broke up the eighth wonder of the world, the Beatles – finally made the list in 1972. Yoko was incredibly unique, a genius, or a pop art fraud only interested in making money – take your pick. The opinions were as varied as her various incarnations: aristocrat, hippie, seer, singer, artist, peace advocate, and wife of John Lennon. Yoko did have one singular force to her multifaceted personality: her wardrobe was out of some opium-induced Easternized nightmare. We were lucky, though, when she wore her basically boring all-white getups or her black Vampirella capes, considering her nude "Two Virgins" album cover with husband John in 1968. John said he wanted people to be shocked when they saw the cover; shocked wasn't the word, really. Horrified was more like it. As for Ono in 1972, she had entered her Haunted Black Forest of Hair period. With all that money she still looked like she needed a creme rinse and a cut, preferably "yesterday." Yet dear Yoko was always one for taking a risk, even if it was at her own expense. Rumor had it she considered herself a witch. Well, dress for success, I always say. And she certainly did.

1·9·7·2

10

Totie Fields

The bad-year blimp covered in sequins – looks like a Fourth of July technicolor explosion!

1973

THE ANDROGYNOUS look hit its gender-bender peak with the emergence of one David Bowie, man of a thousand faces, a thousand voices. Suddenly, makeup for men became an avant-garde fad for the truly hip – or desperate, depending on your point of view. But Bowie's entrance into the fashionable world of rock foreshadowed literally dozens of fads to follow, prompting him to say, looking back on those trendsetting days in the early seventies, "They keep recycling *all* of us . . . which is *great*. I think that's fabulous." Well, I prefer to be kind and call Bowie eccentric. The fashions he inspired certainly were that, if not downright berserk. After the fashion rebellion of the sixties, I was prepared for anything – until I saw David Bowie in 1973.

In less controversial territory, the craze for pants became almost too boring to bitch about. I had other fish to fry, beginning with the fabric that wouldn't die, used on endless garments from slacks to dresses to jackets to coats: denim. I was literally drowning in a sea of blue denim, as waves of accompanying halter tops, tank tops, and T-shirts emblazoned with all kinds of cute phrases crashed around my head. The natural, relaxed mood was popular with the youth market, and denim leveled the pretensions of certain classes of society almost instantly. When blue-blooded dowagers (whose only contact with blue jeans was

② Princess Anne

Makes her mother, The Queen, look fashionable!

③ Raquel Welch
1·9·7·3

Trying to keep abreast of the times, with those clothes, is hard!

④ Billie Jean King
1·9·7·3

What a racket – with backhand fashion!

⑤ Jacqueline Onassis
1·9·6·0

If pants are in, she will put them out!

thirty years ago when they once saw a gardener from a terrace window) started jumping into jeans, I knew we were in serious fashion-clone territory. As far as denim goes, we still are.

Adding to the overuse of sweaters in 1972, the legendary cardigan was back – cable knit in white or pale beige bordered with rows of bright stripes. America was dotted with lots of would-be tennis players as the cardigan quickly became the hottest accessory of the year, followed by the perfect fall fashion coda: the Gatsby look, with its ultra-romantic chiffons and pastel silk cocktail dresses. The Jazz Age, if only for a moment, was back. I actually liked the low-waisted, slightly bloused silhouettes I saw. Anything was better than tank tops and jeans – 1973's unfortunate fashion obsession.

A brand-new star shot right up to the number one spot in 1973. Everything about divine diva Bette Midler, including her outrageous outfits, electrified. I first saw Midler when she and I shared the dais on the Johnny Carson show. The minute the flame-haired typhoon swept on stage I knew she was going to be a superstar – perhaps even, in time, a legend. She was absolutely fabulous, furiously gifted, unbelievably funny, and wore clothes that were nearly indescribable in their truly tacky aura of bosom-baring, fanny-wagging exhibitionism. Midler was like no one before her, except perhaps Carmen Miranda crossed with Judy Garland and Sophie Tucker, with a dollop of Edith Piaf thrown in for good measure. To concentrate on her fashions was, even to me, almost missing the point, but offstage she looked even worse: a polyester-print grab bag of fashion dementia topped off with a mass of carrot curls that resembled Little Orphan Annie as interpreted by Salvador Dali. She was beyond camp. She seemed to reinvent it in her own irascible yet lovable image. She once wrote, "**** 'em if they can't take a joke." Need I say more?

The Andrews Sisters – whom Midler paid tribute to by reviving a raucous version of "Boogie Woogie Bugle Boy" in her act – multiplied the musical madness of fashion failure times three. The triplicate of terror was enough to frighten even the most hardened couture critic. They managed to stop the Chattanooga Choo-Choo dead in its tracks.

Liv Ullman, queen of the Bergmanesque psychodramas that make you want to slit your wrists after five minutes in the theatre, took

1·9·7·3

6

Elke Sommer

A do-it-yourself kit with the wrong instructions!

Sarah Miles

1·9·7·3

7

Did she buy her wardrobe in a blackout?

> "*I never wore dresses as much as Milton Berle did.*"
> – 1973 LISTMAKER DAVID BOWIE TO *ROLLING STONE*
>
> "*Once is enough . . . when you're Ziggy Stardust.*"
> – MR. BLACKWELL

Andrews Sisters

"Boogie Woogie Bugle Boy" on an old clothes line!

her drab, desperate, dowdy look home from the set. What a saga of somber seriousness Ullman was! I felt like I needed to see a therapist just to qualify for criticizing her. Her emergence into Hollywood – with the superbomb *Lost Horizon* musical as her dubious debut – was short-lived, prompting Bette Midler to joke, "I never miss a Liv Ullman musical!" Maybe she didn't, but everybody else did.

David Bowie became the first man since Uncle Miltie to hit the list. One of the biggest trendsetters of the seventies, Bowie – especially in his Ziggy Stardust drag – defied description in mere earthly terms. As a space oddity he was mesmerizing; as a fashion oddity he was equally successful, especially with the Day-Glo makeup.

Liv Ullman

Will the real thrift shop stand up?

David Bowie

A cross between Joan Crawford and Marlene Dietrich doing a glitter revival of *New Faces*!

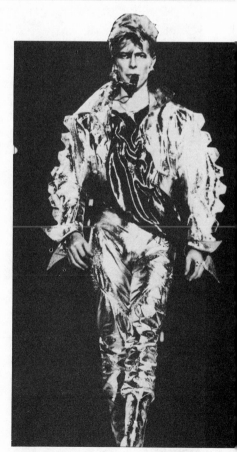

1974

MORE THAN EVER BEfore, I went on a rampage in 1974. Although fashion had threatened to destroy itself in the past, I finally had to admit it was dead. After all, it's quite simple: make a woman look as ugly as possible and she'll stop buying. And they did – in droves. Women were left stranded between halter horrors and jeweled jeans.. Little else was available because most designers were out to lunch, aesthetically. When they did manage to return to their drawing boards, symptoms of indigestion must have colored their work. What else can explain the monstrosities thrust upon us all?

The only real news was the return of the cape, created and immortalized by Pauline Trigère, Seventh Avenue's baroness of fashion. For the tall and slim, the cape was a dramatic special effect; for most women, however, the look was batlike. Capes did serve an important purpose in 1974 – they managed to cover up the nightmares underneath. For that I was grateful.

Lounging pajamas were popular as were swirling floor-length slacks. Boots were still in vogue, but mercifully, softer, daintier shoes – T-straps and ankle straps with delicate details – returned. The clog was nearly over; heels were high and slim, perhaps to make the bulky above-the-waist cape fiasco even more ridiculous to the eye. The balance was all wrong, like most everything else.

Jeans endured like the plague. Hats, belts, scarves, and mufflers showed up as did the rolled brim hat, which people like Bella Abzug took to extreme outer limits. She, like most others, didn't need an umbrella. The overextended brim was enough.

Silver jewelry was back, in keeping with the nonglamour, nodazzle styles wasting away on the showroom racks. But a movement was brewing to throw all caution to the wind. It began in the underground clubs of New York and London, and it was dubbed "New Wave." Safety pins would never be the same again.

Fanne Foxe

1·9·7·4 ③

Too much first name showing and "foxing" around the edges!

1·9·7·4 ④

Bella Abzug

A 1940's fashion intellect!

1·9·7·4 ⑤

Cher Bono

Looks like a Hawaiian Bat Mitzvah!

"All I want to do is work, sing . . . and be stupid."
– 1974 LISTMAKER CHER, QUOTED IN ANDY WARHOL'S *EXPOSURES*

" . . . your fashions bare you out."
– MR. BLACKWELL

1974

1·9·7·4

6

Charo

Carmen Miranda with cleavage!

The Pointer Sisters

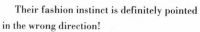

Their fashion instinct is definitely pointed in the wrong direction!

7

1·9·7·4

1·9·7·4

8

Raquel Welch

Still trying – fashion could give her a lift!

The emergence of Cher – the quintessential fashion folly of the seventies (at least) – gave me fuel for the fire like few ever have. It takes real imagination to look this bad. In 1974, Cher was at her navel-bearing nadir in her exploding fireworks of a wardrobe. Just like a cherry bomb, she should have been banned before the rash of imitators took Miss Bono's loco look to the streets. But, of course, there really was only *one* Cher – and for that I suppose we should all be grateful! Cher has had more looks than David Bowie, Elizabeth Taylor, and the Mormon Tabernacle Choir combined – all bad, badder, and baddest. From the gypsy getups (appropriate only when howling at the moon) to the vampy, campy slit-to-hell-and-back evening disasters, Cher singlehandedly brought the glitzed-to-the-tits look back. Or the front. It was hard to tell with her! Surfboards had more curves.

Helen Reddy sang "I Am Woman;" thanks for the warning. The irony of that song was not lost on me. Helen, who, one wag joked, was arrested for loitering onstage, should have been arrested for her shapeless, dull-as-dishwater drabness. Her parade of pantsuits were as vapid as her voice: a litany of low notes nonpareil.

Bella Abzug, with a wardrobe as loud as her mouth, brought oversize hats back from the dead, which is where they should have stayed. Bella – bellicose as ever in a barrage of batty hats as big as a New York borough – believed in wide brims and even wider hips, which she flaunted in below-the-knee 1940s fashion debris. At least you knew she was politically honest – no secret slush funds for her. One look at her clothes proved that fact without a moment's hesitation.

Designer Sonia Rykiel became the first couturier to be honored. Her tributes to the world of design were, among other hopeless styles, epitomized by ankle pants and skeletal silhouettes with muscle-bound prices. In a case of rubbing salt into the wardrobe wound, she appeared everywhere in her unflattering designs that were unwearable to anyone over the age of 20. Obviously, she didn't notice, but I did.

And then there was the "Coochi-Coochi" girl herself – Xavier Cugat's more developed half, Charo. Her clothes were as unfathomable as her accent. Looking like a sequined steroid, she bumped and ground her way straight onto the list. Like an earthquake, Charo was beyond human control or under-standing. Only mother nature was to blame.

1·9·7·4

Karen Valentine

Straight out of a Victorian scrapbook. The "Little Girl" forever!

1·9·7·4

Sonia Rykiel

Makes them, wears them, and that ends fashion!

ONCE AGAIN, MUSIC dominated the fashion industry. New Wave, punk, glitter rock. Sequins were everywhere, even on a few women – but not many.

Despite the plethora of leather, Spandex, and lace on the flamboyant musical trendsetters, mass America watched but didn't wear. What they did wear was denim, now narrow-legged and designed to be worn rolled up to the midcalf, over boots. The farmhand aura was tempered somewhat by the fact that jeans got tighter – to the point of many circulation mishaps and several car wrecks, too. The rear end became the seat of fashion power. Unfortunately, most women stuffed into these insidious body snatchers looked more like bad accidents than traffic-stoppers.

Now denim was prewashed, brushed, streaked, bleached, studded, embroidered, jeweled. In other words, they did everything they could to dress it up but nothing worked. At least not to anyone who preferred Joni James to Joni Mitchell.

The jumper jumped back into the 1975 fashion pit, allowing women to move into dresses and still utilize sweaters and blouses collected – lo so many bad collections ago – as separates.

Sweaters got creative: Mexican, Peruvian, Icelandic, and American Indian motifs decorated cardigans, wrap jackets, and pullovers. But the huge cowl necks that replaced the turtle necks resembled a mangled angora sweater after a bad wash. Then bib overalls became the rage for street fashion – a truly cruel shock to the senses.

1975

For evening, China was the place to be – pure silks in Honan, Shantung, and crash weaves began to appear in designer lines. Straw shoulder bags from mainland China, the summer accessory, were matched with quilted "coolie" jackets and vests with frog closings, mandarin collars, and various other oriental overlays. The geisha girl look – all jade, Chinese red, and cobalt – was stylized, striking, and – let's face it – nearly impossible to wear.

Still, there was a glimmer of hope. By the end of the year, dress sales were on the rise, even if the year's biggest seller was a smock. At least it was a start.

Worst

1 1975

Caroline Kennedy

A shaggy dog in pants!

1·9·7·5

2

Helen Reddy

She spent the year proving I was right. Should have saved her costumes for the bicentennial explosion!

1·9·7·5

③

Nancy
Kissinger

A traveling fashion stew!

Bette Midler 1·9·7·5

④

"Betsy Bloomer" — didn't
pantaloons go out with the hoopskirt?

1975

1·9·7·5

⑤

Sally Struthers

Certainly not in the "Fashion family"!

1975

1·9·7·5

6 *Princess Anne*

A royal auto mechanic!

Tammy Wynette and Donna Fargo **1·9·7·5** **7**

Tied for the yearly double:
country magic dressed in a circus tent!

1·9·7·5 **8** *Tatum O'Neal*

Twelve going on forty!

1·9·7·5 **9** *Sonia Rykiel*

She put the "fanny wrap" back in
and out of fashion!

> *"I want some glamour. Some flash . . .
> things like Cher's."*
> – 1975 LISTMAKER ELTON JOHN, TO
> DESIGNER BOB MACKIE, IN *ROLLING
> STONE*
>
> *"Some nightmares are never ending."*
> – MR. BLACKWELL

In 1975, Elton John craved glamour, and he got it. Like Cher in drag, Elton took sequins, feathers, and furs beyond the realm of mere opulence into Liberace-levels of overstatement heretofore undiscovered. His clothes were outrageous camp doubled and tripled; you worried if he could keep up the pace. To his credit, he always did but he had the smarts to wear sunglasses to shield himself from his walking laser show of a wardrobe. We, however, were defenseless, waiting prey temporarily blinded by Elton's mad assault. In his rhinestoned Bob Mackie jumpsuits, platform shoes two feet high, and neon-lit glasses, Elton was English eccentric personified: a bit of Noel Coward, Paul McCartney, and the Queen mixed up in one horrendous fashion fiasco. Like his compatriot in camp, David Bowie, Elton joined the list in 1975.

Caroline Kennedy seemed to pick up her fashion tips from her mother, and they were all bad. Looking like a refugee from Woodstock, Caroline lived in jeans, cotton tops, and shapeless jackets. Her hair, a wild mass of dull brown frizz, was too long, too shaggy, too hurricane victim for me. Caroline was every badly dressed young woman across America, and rightfully placed number one. Only Helen Reddy, still looking like a feminist fiasco, gave her a run for the money.

Midler was Midler: still tacky, still determined to sink to the lowest taste factor imaginable. Two country and western queens, Tammy Wynette and Donna Fargo, tied for seventh place. "Bargain-basement bonanza" was the only phrase that came to mind when confronted with Donna and Tammy's backwoods bombs. Tammy should have stopped standing by her man and started standing in front of a mirror; she might have saved herself a lot of heartsick blues.

Princess Anne found it next to impossible to stay off the list. In 1975 she was back, a walking, talking wax museum of dowager drag forty years too soon. Anne, who took dowdiness to the same passionate peak Elton John took campy glitter, might have been a born princess, but she achieved her status as fashion pauper on her ornery own.

1·9·7·5

Elton John

Would be the campiest spectacle in the Rose Parade!

IT WAS THE YEAR OF THE remade King Kong, a perfect symbol for the beastly fashion that clasped its hairy hand around the American consumer. It was also the bicentennial year, which meant that everything not nailed to the floor was re-hued in red, white, and blue. I'm as patriotic as the next man, but bicentennial toilet paper was too much even for me. As for the fashions, they were beyond mere patriotism. They were downright hokum that would have made Betsy Ross blush.

1976 did see a positive trend toward dressing up. The "big dress," which de-feminized women to the point of sacklike statements, had narrowed to the "tube" – great if you were bone thin with no excess baggage to claim. That was the problem: there was no in between. Fashion had become a business of extremes – perfect for reviving sagging sales but bad on the busted buyer.

For daywear, the classic haberdashery look was in: sharp, constructed, masculine, and – to me – quite unflattering on the average American woman. After five, the atmosphere im-proved. Soft and sexy came back in a burst of opulent fabrics, beads, and embroidery. Although culottes and harem pants were utilized, tied at the ankle like a court jester expecting a flood, I almost didn't

1976

Worst

1
19 76

Louise Lasser

"Mary Hartman, Mary Hartman" – last summer's "Tumble Weed, Tumble Weed"!

1·9·7·6 **2** *Maralin Niska*

Carmen dressed like Sadie Thompson!

1·9·7·6
③ *Angie Dickinson*
The "Policewoman" that has caught everything but fashion!

1·9·7·6
④ *Charo*
A rumble seat with a pushed-up front!

1·9·7·6
⑤ *Ann Miller*
A 1937 screen test!

I can't believe it!

bother to complain because . . .

The traditional pantsuit was deemed to be *out*. I celebrated by burning old *Women's Wear Daily*'s celebrating the omnipotence of the "trouser suit" for women. Other designs were equally misguided: the tunic top with pants, the return of the kilt – which made every girl a preppy whether she belonged to the Country Club of Virginia or not – and the reemergence of the poncho.

Love beads were over; diamonds were back. Much to my chagrin, they were used to stud ankle bracelets, which just goes to show one never can have it all.

Despite the glimmer of hope in 1976, I feared another disastrous trend beginning to emerge – a trend that would burst into thumping view in 1977. The look was disco; the result was camp Frisco at best.

1·9·7·6
6
Queen Juliana

All the queen's horses and all the queen's men couldn't make Julie look good again!

 1·9·7·6
7
Lee Radziwill

Did Lee's designer go down with the *Titanic*?

1·9·7·6
8
Loretta Lynn

The right dress in the wrong century!

1·9·7·6
9
Nancy Walker

Vacuum cleaners have better covers!

1·9·7·6
10
Dinah Shore

Wild again, beguiled again, and constantly contrived again!

The year's hippest, hottest show, "Mary Hartman, Mary Hartman," a brilliant satire on suburban life in America, showcased the quirky talents of Mary Kay Place, Dodie Goodman, and number one Listmaker Louise Lasser. Starring as Mary Hartman, Louise was a zonked-out housewife with a perpetually glazed stare, dealing with a loony bin of bizarre neighbors and surreal relatives. Off the set, Louise was equally eccentric. Nothing she wore matched, fit, or made any sense whatsoever. Like her good friend Woody Allen, Lasser made insecurity a personal style and statement – and dressed accordingly. Baggy tops, baggy bottoms, baggy coats – Louise looked like a therapist's nightmare. The odd, occasional touch of lace Lasser employed only widened the gap of her schizophrenic fashion image. What is it about Woody Allen, anyway? Three of his companions, Mia Farrow, Louise Lasser, and Diane Keaton, have all reached lofty peaks on my annual list. He must be attracted to women who look worse than he does. Difficult, but obviously not impossible.

Another bright television star, Angie Dickinson, was decidedly dim in the wardrobe department. As the little screen's favorite policewoman, Angie looked bad enough to be booked as a public nuisance. Despite a beautiful face and the best legs in the world, Angie did everything she could to make herself look as cheap as possible: directionless hair, gaudy nighttime disasters, skintight jeans. Not a heartwarming sight, but certainly a stomach-turning one.

Dinah Shore – one of the few stars who would really like to see me buried under the state of Tennessee in a cement box – returned in flowery fashion force in 1976. With her solid and print pantsuits, in ice-cream colors that very nearly glowed in the dark, Dinah's wardrobe was shakier than her vibrato. And as outdated.

Three other singers – Maralin Niska, the opera diva; Charo, the Vegas vixen; and Ann Miller, the MGM matriarch – dressed in the same musical mayhem of too much, too late, while Loretta Lynn entered new regions of bad retro prairie garb. Still stuck on the front porch of country fashion, Lynn dressed like the Queen of the Square Dance. Extravagant hokum, at least.

Queen Juliana and Princess Lee Radziwill proved a silver-spoon life-style is no advantage in the Best Dressed department. Juliana and Lee, born into the sequestered social filigree of frivolity, were slaves to bad taste and style. They looked about as elegantly regal as a plastic fork on a paper plate.

> *"We both . . . had the same sense of the ridiculous."*
> – LISTMAKER LEE RADZIWILL, ON A CERTAIN SIMILARITY WITH SISTER JACKIE O, IN *ONE SPECIAL SUMMER.*
>
> *"Especially in designers."*
> – MR. BLACKWELL

1977

△ **1**

1977

Farrah Fawcett-Majors

Enough splits in her dress for an earthquake!

▽ **2**

1·9·7·7

Linda Ronstadt

Bought her entire wardrobe during a five-minute bus stop!

3 1·9·7·7 *Charo*

Coochi, Coochi . . . is that a dress or a bug killer?

Anita Bryant

△ **4** 1·9·7·7

She should go to the "Queen's" dressmaker!

△ **5** 1·9·7·7

Diane Keaton

Ash-can fashions from her local alley!

1977

1·9·7·7

Dolly Parton

Scarlett O'Hara dressed like Mae West in *My Little Chickadee*!

IN APRIL OF 1977, STUDIO 54 opened its haughty doors in New York City, and the disco era was born. Originally an opera house (fate is a cruel thing), the cavernous, multileveled theatre with its red velvet balconies reigned supreme as the hottest, hippest, most fashionable fantasyland in America. A cross section of superstars in haute couture, models in faded jeans, dowagers in Fendi furs, punks in Harry Winston diamonds, and hedonists with "Nuclear War – What About My Career?" logos emblazoned on ripped T-shirts typified the glitter/trash/post-Warhol/gay/straight/bi/tri/black/white/red/green crowds that swirled under the rainbow lights to Donna Summer, Gloria Gaynor, and Diana Ross anthems. Studio 54 was an important cultural melting pot; fashions worn there spread to cities across America. We were at the pretentious peak of the "Me" decade. Self-absorption was at its height, but with all that self-involvement and self-obsession going on, it's funny how grotesque most of the disco-goers looked. It makes one wonder what all those fabulous faces *really* thought about themselves. Judging from their outfits, not very much. Ah yes, the sixties were definitely over.

In the real world – if in 1977 there really was one – fashion took the glitter look to national saturation levels. "Trash/flash" was everywhere, from evening lingerie, split skirts, one-piece tubes, see-through blouses, even socks and stockings, to sequin-strewn shoes and boots. The circus look was back and bigger than ever, all set to the strains of "I Will Survive." I certainly hoped so, but those tieless three-piece suits so conducive to "discoitis" were positively fatal.

Fashion's split personality juxtaposed itself like never before in 1977. On one hand, the disco drag was beyond hot; on the other, the *Annie Hall* layered laundry bag attitude was becoming big news, too. Like urban gypsies, the Annie Halls mixed and matched chino pants with skinny ties, baggy coats with serpentine-hemmed midis, bulky sweaters with bulky vests. The Annie Halls were masters of camouflage – one had no idea where the body began and the thirty layers of monochromatic fabric ended. This said something about insecurity, but I'm no psychiatrist. Wearing these raggy coverups would, though, only seem to inflame an already deranged psyche.

Kenzo introduced what looked like a sheet worn sideways as the big new "wrap" of the year. Castelbajac brought out huge hooded one-piece coats more suitable for a monastery than America in 1977. Shawls were hot. The look was not.

73

Marie Osmond 1·9·7·7 **7**

Overdone and overdressed; "The Good Ship Lollipop" in dry dock!

1·9·7·7 **9** Chris Evert

If tailored is in . . . so is boring!

1·9·7·7 **8** Dyan Cannon

Looks like she was blown out of one in a circus!

NOTES of INTEREST

Toothy, blonde, beautiful Farrah Fawcett-Majors, star of "Charlie's Angels" and *the* poster that sent one-piece bathing suit sales into the stratosphere, grinned her way onto the list without mussing one hair on her blow-dried-to-death head. Farrah was into the Studio 54 slit-skirt, cave-woman look. Watching her desecrate herself was enough to make me want to slit my wrists. Or at least send her a seamstress to sew up the rips that ravaged her wardrobe.

Diane Keaton – the original Annie Hall – brought neurotic chic into vogue. Her loony collection of thrift shop hand-me-downs, which she must have bought and worn by the pound, were a tribute to clutter, and not much else.

Miss Marie Osmond of the singing Osmonds desperately needed fashion guidance in 1977. Like a road show version of Cher, Marie was less vulgar but equally as overglitzed and overwrought. Everything about Marie was too perfect, too coiffed, too too – a definite overreaction from being the only girl in a bevy of boys. She was Shirley Temple in sequins, and the effect was a lot more saccharine than stunning.

Songstresses Linda Ronstadt and Dolly Parton were image opposites, but still received similar fashion points for being hopelessly out of style. Linda was a Malibu canyon kind of girl. Dressed in jeans and T-shirts, she was a rock n' roll recipe for dull, drab, and dreary. The queen of the hillbillies had a few hills and valleys of her own, and Dolly Parton took great delight in exposing every acre possible – ravines and all. Dolly was beyond description with her mile-high dimestore wigs, mile-low cowgirl extravaganzas rhinestoned to the point of klieg-light intensity, and hourglass figure corseted torture-chamber tight. To paraphrase a popular slogan for the movie *Willard*, where your sequined nightmares end, Dolly Parton begins.

Charo continued her reign of fashion terror, while Dyan Cannon – she of the cackle-for-days laugh – should have stopped shrieking long enough to look in the mirror. If she had, she might have been a little less pleased with herself. The rest of the world certainly was.

1·9·7·7

10

Margaret Trudeau

Canada's loss is New York's loss!

THE REVOLVING DOOR of frenetic fads was busy in 1978. Now, the "big dress" was deemed passé. Glamour with a capital *G* was back and I, for one, was ecstatic. Someone had woken up on Seventh Avenue after a very long nap, and for the first time in what seemed to be a lifetime, beautiful clothes started showing up again. Fashion moves in trends and 1978 was a positive one. I didn't want to think about the longevity of this sudden stroke of good luck; after all, one moment of bliss is worth a year of Pucci prints.

Joan Crawford-style gowns were introduced. The inverted wedge was *the* new shape. Black satins and velvets, higher heels, and long, fitted skirts topped with slightly broader shoulders (*not* the *Bride of Frankenstein* football-sized pads of the 1980's) looked regal, elegant, and chic.

Now for the bad news. For everyday wear, the jogging suit was a national mania. From the sublime to the ridiculous in less than twenty-four hours was too much of a change for me, especially since the outfit in question looked more like a reject from *Bozo the Clown* than anything else. The real irony is that, for the most part, the women that stuffed themselves into their lime green running suits had never seen a track in their lives. Most of their exercise had involved walking to the refrigerator, toning up by balancing Breyer's bricks, and cooling down with a banana split. Still, the jogging suit covered a multitude of caloric sins, which was the real fashion statement that the jogging suit made anyway.

Jeans were paired with full, silky blouses with plunging

Dolly Parton

Too many yards of Dolly poured into too few inches of fabric!

1978

necklines. No worse, no better than any other look associated with denim. All of it was pretty mundane, and too boring to elaborate on. Other mistakes of 1978 included the "grandpa" oversize shirt with narrow collar band and the loose chemise worn over cigarette pants. String bikinis separated the women from the toothpicks while accessories such as jewelry continued the infinitesimal, less is less mentality. Stick pins, tiny earrings, little brooches; give me a row of cabochon rubies any day. Hair fashions ranged from the banana roll to "after punk"; lace, veils, hats, and gloves returned. But, as usual in the right-idea-at-the-wrong-time syndrome of the 1970s, they were worn most often in smokey discos – a waste of glamour if there ever was one.

2 · 1·9·7·8
Suzanne Somers
Looks like she was hit by a flash flood!

3 · 1·9·7·8
Christina Onassis Kavzov
Mother Earth is playing Russian roulette with her wardrobe!

Cheryl Tiegs
4 · 1·9·7·8
The three T's — Tiegs, Tacky, Togs. A moulting road runner!

5 · 1·9·7·8
Farrah Fawcett-Majors
Strikes a minor cord in fashion.

1978

1·9·7·8
6
Queen Noor
A centerfold for *Popular Mechanics!*

1·9·7·8
7
Olivia Newton-John
The right dress in the wrong century.

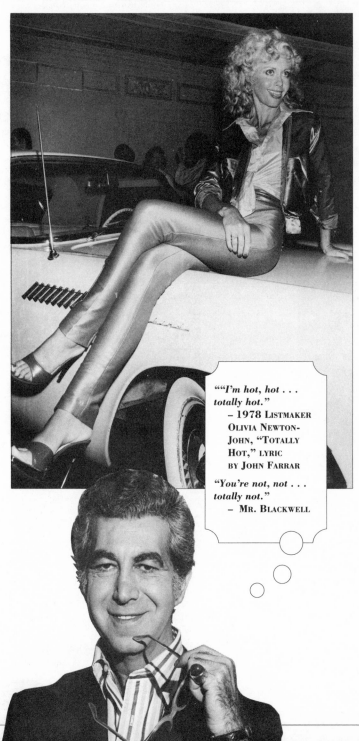

"*"I'm hot, hot . . . totally hot."*
– 1978 LISTMAKER
OLIVIA NEWTON-
JOHN, "TOTALLY
HOT," LYRIC
BY JOHN FARRAR

"You're not, not . . . totally not."
– MR. BLACKWELL

NOTES of INTEREST

No longer did the stars of cinema and music monopolize the myriad mistakes of bad wardrobe habits. Television was rapidly becoming *the* hot spot for potential Listmakers. Television mirrored mass society the way films rarely could, and the fashion influence was enormous. Farrah Fawcett's lioness mane, for example, copied by every subpar beauty shop assistant this side of Kalamazoo, became the "mane" event to girls from six to sixty. And her clothes, or lack thereof, were emulated by all the wrong people – and bodies. To put it bluntly, Farrah was a hymn to cheap, but women fell for her Vegas look hook, line, and halter. The look was laughable – just like those other comedy television queens, Suzanne Somers, Penny Marshall, and Cindy Williams. Offscreen they elicited more tears than smiles in the fashion script of their lives; no happy ending in view.

"Three's Company" Suzanne Somers knew as much about couture as Minnie Mouse. Awash in tight beaded dresses for evening – more squashed than posh – Suzanne either needed to lose ten pounds or consider reupholstering her posterior in a fabric that wasn't reminiscent of spray paint.

Penny Marshall and Cindy Williams of "Laverne and Shirley"

were 1950s fashion flops in the hit ABC comedy. The look worked in the context of the show; in the context of real life, however, Penny's dressed-for-the-bowling-alley-getups and Cindy's "little miss mediocre" suburban skirts and blouses were about as exciting as a bowl of leftover tapioca pudding. Without the raisins, but lumpy as hell.

All-American fashion model personified, the sunshiny Cheryl Tiegs was a hideous hurricane of overlapping styles, looks, and ideas in 1978. Obviously being the most famous model in the world had little effect on her fashion sense; perhaps being inundated daily with hundreds of garments confused her sense of equilibrium. At least I hope that's her excuse.

Christina Onassis proved that all the Swiss bank accounts in the world can't finance good taste. Christina was a sinking super-tanker of excess, an epic Greek tragedy of Olympian opulence to the point of overkill. The unfortunate fact that she maintained a poor hound-dog expression most of the time only underscored her obvious discomfort with her image.

And then there was number one Listmaker Dolly Parton – the leaning hourglass of Pisa, Southern style.

⑧ Cindy Williams and Penny Marshall

Double-feature disaster!

1·9·7·8

⑨ Linda Ronstadt

Hits a high note in song, but a low note in fashion.

Bette Midler ⑩

1·9·7·8

She didn't go to a rummage sale, she wore it!

Bo Derek

The "love" child of the eighties
gets a minus 10 for fashion!

Jill Clayburgh **2** 1·9·7·9

Dresses like an African bush . . .
waiting for her safari!

1·9·7·9 **3**

Loni Anderson

Gravity could be her worst enemy, and she
dresses to prove it!

1979

1·9·7·9 **4**

Christina Onassis

Dressed to check
her oil tankers!

THANK GOD THE SEVENties were almost over. Tennessee Williams once was asked what he did during the decade and he responded "I slept." A perfect response to a forgettable period in American history, not to mention fashion infamy. First Lady Rosalyn Carter – whom I have tried to avoid mentioning up till now – epitomized the dressed-down-to-the-point-of-evaporation look that infiltrated most of the decade. Yes, glitter did thrive as did a brief resurgence of glamour in 1978, but for the most part the seventies were the nadir of design creativity.

In 1979, the industry bade farewell to the ethnic era. More sophisticated silhouettes began appearing with wide shoulders tapering to the hem. Slit skirts and spike heels exaggerated the look of 1978 beyond tasteful recognition.

Black velvet was the fabric for dressy jackets; unfortunately they were paired with silly knicker suits worn with white ruffled shirts. I thought we were having a revival of the Paul Revere and the Raiders syndrome until someone pointed out that Paul Revere wouldn't be caught dead wearing knit.

Tartan skirts, plaid shirts, and satin trousers were hot, and for once the waist was the fashion focal point. Silk cummerbunds were worn. On the right figure the look was smashing; on the wrong one, images of a modern-day Sinbad the Sailor sprang to mind.

Pants – believe it or not – got even tighter. The posterior was positively showcased in spray-painted denim, while jump shorts with wide elasticized belts were popular for roller skating. Oh, please. The look wasn't fit for the roller derby, much less a roller rink.

Down jackets, which resembled enlarged life preservers, were the preppy rage. The bohemians wore oversize shirts tied in a knot at the waist. Whatever your social affiliation, there was a look of equivalent terror for everyone. For once, the fashion industry was an equal opportunity employer.

Deborah (Blondie) Harry

Ten cents a dance
with a nickel in change!

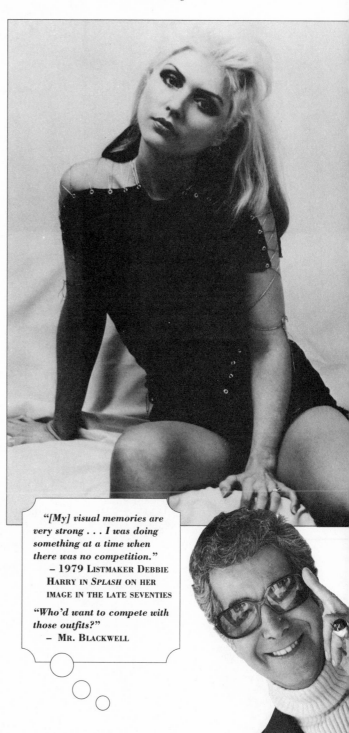

"[My] visual memories are very strong . . . I was doing something at a time when there was no competition."
– 1979 LISTMAKER DEBBIE HARRY IN SPLASH ON HER IMAGE IN THE LATE SEVENTIES

"Who'd want to compete with those outfits?"
– MR. BLACKWELL

1979

1·9·7·9 **6** *Dolly Parton*

A ruffled bedspread
covering king-size pillows!

Mayor Dianne Feinstein 1·9·7·9 **7**

Looks like she is
wearing the voting
booth!

1·9·7·9 **8** *Princess Margaret*

Most women dress to
disguise their age . . .
Princess Margaret
dresses to prove it!

1·9·7·9 **9** *Valerie Perrine*

Looks like the *Bride
of Frankenstein* doing
the Ziegfeld Follies!

The hottest star in the country, Bo Derek, eclipsed Farrah Fawcett as everyone's favorite nubile nymph. As the fantasy-come-to-life girl of Dudley Moore's dreams in Blake Edwards' smash *10*, Miss Derek was reminiscent of a young Ursula Andress or a teenage Linda Evans. This did not go unnoticed by her husband John, who was married to Bo's older lookalikes several bad seasons before he met Bo on a beach somewhere and married her. Bo's look was 1960s kitsch: cluttered, ill fitting, and ill advised. She seemed to strive toward looking as unglamorous as possible, and her corn-row catastrophe of a hairstyle was more reminiscent of shock treatment than a fashion statement. Needless to say, she wasn't a ten on my list; she made it all the way to number one.

1·9·7·9

10

Margaux Hemingway

A Hanukkah bush the day after Christmas!

Debbie Harry – one of the original glitter punkers of the mid-seventies – had finally catapulted to national acclaim with her group Blondie. Looking like an Andy Warhol fantasy, Debbie brought punk into the mainstream. The water got polluted faster than the guitar riffs that rattled through her music.

Princess Margaret returned in fashion shame in 1979. Gone were the more contemporary clothes she once perpetrated on a horrified public. In their place were a series of grand dame, dowdy, dullsville dresses and coats that were as depressing as the London fog.

Christina Onassis continued her reign as the international bow-wow of the year, while Dolly Parton was back bigger than ever in her Smoky Mountain monstrosities.

San Francisco mayor Dianne Feinstein obviously did not take advantage of the city's most creative fashion talent. Boxy suits, dark unflattering colors, and matronly skirts looked more like a windy wardrobe catastrophe in Chicago than an attempt at elegance and style in the City by the Bay. As mayor, I suppose her advisors told her to embrace conservatism; in the city of Haight-Ashbury, flower power, Rice-a-roni, and cable cars, Dianne was a monument to boredom – not indicative of San Francisco in the least.

Valerie Perrine, who emerged as 1974's new sex kitten in Bob Fosse's *Lenny*, was 1979's sex hex. What she did to clothes only Houdini could figure out.

The

EIGHTIES

Brooke Shields

Looks like a Halloween trick without the treat!

1·9·8·0
2

Elizabeth Taylor

Forever Amber in drag!

1·9·8·0
3

Suzanne Somers

Recycled spaghetti!

Bo Derek

A butterfly wearing her cocoon!

1·9·8·0
4

> *"I'm an old bag."*
> – 1980 Listmaker
> Elizabeth Taylor, quoted in
> Dick Sheppard's *Elizabeth*
>
> *"She said it, not me!"*
> – Mr. Blackwell

1980

T HE 1980s WOULD grow to symbolize the return to glamour, glitz, and Reagan red. As the year began, style and elegance were on their way, but hadn't arrived quite yet. President Carter still ruled the country in a sea of down-home cardigans while Rosalyn continued her hopeless attempts to set some sort of style for herself. Like the election, she lost.

The biggest fad before the Reagan revolution hit was the "walking sleeping bag." Nylon down-filled garments in dizzying colors, like waterlogged garbage bags, stalked the streets. Unsightly and unbecoming on anyone claiming to be a member of the female gender, these were the last gasps of antifeminine fashion looks before Mrs. Reagan began buying new china for the trip back east.

We were seeing the end (thank you) of the obligatory pants and knit top combination, but the beginning of a craze toward country and western duds. Fringe, moccasins, beaded headbands, and Bo Derek's corn-row hairstyle ballooned to national saturation points. Jangling bracelets by the dozen were worn, as were string ties and wide silver-studded belts. The effect was Square Dance Personified with a little Pocahontas thrown in for ethnic authenticity. Although many women believed their infatuation with country and western /

1·9·8·0 ⑤
Charlene "Dallas" Tilton

A pin-up for Fredericks of Hollywood!

American Indian styles was an homage to the past, most resembled an homage to "Custer's Last Stand". There was a very good reason the cowboy look went out with the Wild Wild West. I saw no reason to bring it back.

For everyday, the T-shirt dress – another fashion loser in a long list of unsightly flops – was the costume. Prints proliferated. Patterns pummeled the senses. Piping peaked. Who cared? Not me. The look was bombsville at best with zero imagination.

As winter approached, the broad shoulder line was emphasized on mannish topcoats with thick padding. The preppy look continued its strict regimen of plaid kilts, wrap-around skirts, kelly green sweaters, and straight coverup dresses. No cleavage for these Junior Leaguers. For evening, black and white was forever – silk blouses in white and cream were paired with black velvet skirts and suits, stockings, and pumps. I felt as if I were living in a silent movie.

1980

1·9·8·0
8 Nancy Lopez
A swinging fashion tragedy!

1·9·8·0
7 Susan Anton
Looks like an ad for a swap meet!

1·9·8·0
9 Princess Grace
Dowdy, not royal!

NOTES of INTEREST

Elizabeth Taylor was back, and bigger than ever. Having become a senator's wife in 1978, Elizabeth had lost all sense of self-restraint and self-respect trapped in Virginia on hubby John Warner's gray stone farm. She was a symphony of caftans, huge flowered shifts, and beaded muu-muu's, loaded down with more jewelry than twelve Vegas showgirls. Horrified Liz-watchers commented that they had wanted all their lives to look like Elizabeth Taylor – and now they did. It was not meant to be a compliment.

Number one on the list, little Miss Brooke Shields of *Pretty Baby* fame, had grown up to be an exquisite beauty and a gawky, incomprehensible fashion mistake. Brooke, although only fifteen, dressed as if she were 40. Rumor had it her mother, Terri, was very protective of Brooke's image. But after *Pretty Baby* and her roundup of fashion bombs, it made you wonder.

The three blonde bombshells – Suzanne Somers, Bo Derek, and Susan Anton – continued their Worst Dressed legacy in cheap clothes that showed either too much or too little. Suzanne and Susan took sequins, cut-to-hell-and-back gowns, and split skirts to the limits. If they had a dollar for every inch of skin they exposed to a panting public in 1980, they'd never have to play Tahoe again. Bo Derek – who didn't need to titillate to wow anyone with 20/20 vision – dressed down. Too down. Swathed in the leather and fringe cowgirl catastrophes so popular with the pseudo rodeo circuit, Bo, believe it or not, nearly pulled it off – but not quite. But her face was perfection. No demented designer could desecrate that. Like Elizabeth Taylor's eyes, some things are beyond reproach.

The era of "Dallas" was beginning. Unfortunately, Charlene Tilton's fashion integrity was ending. As Lucy Ewing, Charlene was a spoiled ball of Texas fire. Off the set Charlene was Hollywood Boulevard bizarre.

And royalty fared no better. Princess Grace of Monaco and Queen Beatrix suddenly looked very bad – and very matronly in the most dowdy manner possible. The princess of Provo, Utah, Marie Osmond, overloaded on wardrobe wattage to the point of fashion meltdown.

1·9·8·0

10

Marie Osmond

Someone should unplug this Christmas tree!

Barbara Mandrell

Yukon Sally playing the Alamo!

1·9·8·1 **2** ## Lynn Redgrave

In knickers her knees look like knockers!

Dolly Parton
3 1·9·8·1

An atomic jelly bean explosion!

Elizabeth Taylor
4 1·9·8·1

She should give up looking for a designer and find an architect!

1

9

1981 FORMALLY ushered in the Reagan era, typified by beads, bows, haute couture, and a return to elegance not seen since the early sixties, when Jackie Kennedy dictated styles from cloth coats to pillbox hats. Suddenly it was okay to bring the sables out of the closet, slip into drop-dead jeweled originals that cost more than many Americans' annual salary, and take the little Chanel and Scaasi suits off their quilted hangers. Opulence – stylish, elegant opulence, not

the Vegas kind – was back. And the color was Nancy Reagan red, red, red – regally patriotic, bold, and rich.

Across the seas, another super-blitz of glitz occurred in July: the marriage of Prince Charles and Lady Diana Spencer. Between Nancy and Di, the globe was swamped in social style and effete extravagance.

The pantsuit was definitely a remnant of the past. Dresses were *de riguer*; hemlines strayed slightly above the knee. Femininity was redefined in subtle yet dazzling

8

1

evening wear. In London, the punk look was wiped off the face of Fleet Street coverage, and designers began a revival of romance. Spurred on by Diana, the Chelsea world went super "Baroque-Grace"; lacy frills, velvet, and huge satin sashes swept through Annabel's and Claridge's every night.

In Washington, D.C., the look was equally ravishing: formal, exquisitely tailored, and designed glamour gowns dotted Capitol Hill's swank party scene. Ruffled taffeta, silk brocade, and embroi-

dered velvet were just three of endless extravagant combinations.

In the fall, the unfortunate penchant for the knicker look proved to be a major sore spot in what otherwise was an exceptional year in fashion. The Little Lord Fauntleroy look was beyond bad; it was strange, nearly surreal, satire.

In accessories from shoes to handbags to belts to jewelry to makeup, the look was gold – preferably 24 carat. Anything less was positively un-Republican.

1981

5

Bernadette Peters

A kinked and curled
kewpie doll on a hayride!

Charlene Tilton **6**
1·9·8·1

Looks like Mount St. Helens erupting!

1·9·8·1

7

Loretta Lynn

Up the music charts, down the fashion charts!

Jane Seymour 1·9·8·1

8

Fashions by medflies!

1·9·8·1

9

Elizabeth Emanuel

Cinderella's stepsister waiting at the
palace gate

NOTES of INTEREST

Barbara Mandrell broke Dolly Parton's run as the worst dressed country and western singer on the planet. Or, perhaps, the universe. Barbara was nice enough to invite me on her television show to pay me back. The gambit backfired – she looked worse than ever. Mandrell, awash in more fussy glitter than Ann Miller in an MGM musical, was unbelievably, undeniably cartoon camp. She made Dolly Parton look almost simple.

Almost being the operative word. Owing to the Mandrell mishaps that grew progressively worse in direct proportion with her rising fame, Miss Parton had dropped to number three. Still, Dolly was horrific; with her Mae West cleavage undraped à la Jayne Mansfield on a very desperate day, Dolly dumbfounded. Truly, a visual only appreciated by the state fair, traveling circus contingent.

Newcomer Lynn Redgrave, who obviously had bad fashion in her genes (sis Vanessa hit the skids twice in her checkered past) definitely disinherited her fashion sense in 1981. Lynn had embraced the knicker fad for fall – and fall she did. Lynn's knees were not her best feature; in fact, pine knobs were smoother in texture. With typical British abandon, Lynn was simply a styleless sin.

Regulars Charlene Tilton and Elizabeth Taylor were too short and plump to wear the cluttered hurricane of hellish garments they chose to stuff themselves into. Garish and gauche, there seemed to be little hope of salvation for these two.

Pop sensation Sheena Easton was a fashion failure. Tiny, delicate, and strikingly beautiful, Sheena dressed more like the Queen of the Jungle than the latest queen of modern music. With a talent for emphasizing all her worst features, Sheena looked like a stuffed cabbage set to a boring backbeat.

And then there was Loretta Lynn. The coal miner's daughter was a fashion masochist's horror in her pizza parlor checks and picnic-table-sized skirts. Loretta was too commanding a woman to settle for a 1950's version of Little Bo Peep, but settle she did – at number seven, without a bullet.

1·9·8·1
10
Sheena Easton

1981

A London roadrunner dressed for the fog!

"I just love Barbra Streisand!"
– 1981 LISTMAKER SHEENA EASTON

"A bad fashion influence if there ever was one. I had a feeling we were going to be seeing a lot of Sheena - and I was right."
– MR. BLACKWELL

Princess Diana

Shy Di has invaded
Queen Victoria's attic!

19

THE FIRST LADY OF fashion, Nancy Reagan, fell victim to the knicker flu that swept the country. In June, at a reception given on the occasion of the Versailles summit, Nancy wore rhinestone-trimmed black satin knickers that knocked her fashion image back a few Givenchys or two. The style peaked with Mrs. Reagan's faux pas. People saw how juvenile knickers really looked and, thankfully, stuffed them away in the out-of-date closet – by now literally brimming with fashion relics of designing dementia.

Another candidate for the closet-of-crap distinction was 1982's hottest fad, the revitalized poncho. Like man-eating moths out of a Stephen King nightmare, the giant shawls took flight over the winter street scene. In basic black – for the bat-girl look – or in muted plaids or bold florals, the poncho was everywhere. Fringed, embroidered, or studded with streaks of metallic thread, the poncho pummeled elegance and creativity to the ground while stimulating Wicked-Witch-of-the-West fantasies in all of us forced to watch.

As a reaction to the knicker – and its use of more leg than the standard pantsuit – dresses were shorter and sexier, often cuffed in a bubble fashion. Pert little hats were used as accessories, signaling the look was more of an ill-timed joke than a serious attempt at style. Still, the rising hemline was very much in the news as snappy, knee-level skirts accompanied the new Spencer suit jacket. Completed by a silk blouse with a ruffle-trimmed high neckline and topped with a mannish slouch hat, the young female executive uniform was simple, chic, and hard as nails. Suit materials were borrowed from men's wardrobes, which further butched up the arid atmosphere. Leather gloves completed the Helmut Newton-like effect.

The Valley Girl look – popularized by such mall queens as Moon Unit Zappa – was "grody to the max." No one could understand a word of their conversations and their sense of style was equally inexplicable. Short skirts with full, blousy tops were accented with ballet slippers. Like neon-colored bag ladies under the influence of American Express, the bitchin' Valley Girls were suburban revenge personified.

1·9·8·2 **2** *Bonnie Franklin*
Not Charlie's aunt, but aunt Charlie!

Victoria Principal 1·9·8·2 **3**
A Dallas Valley Girl!

1·9·8·2 **4** *Bette Midler*
Second-Hand Rose after a hurricane!

1982

 5 *Charlene Tilton*

A Victorian lampshade holding her breath!

Christina Onassis **6**

Daddy's tanker!

7 *Princess Yasmin Aga Khan*

A preppy gypsy!

Jan Stephenson **8**

Mrs. Miniver in a tutu!

9 *Cathy Lee Crosby*

It looks as if she bought out a rummage sale, wore it all, and . . . that's incredible!

> *"What makes a man, what makes a woman, what is gender?"*
> — 1982 LISTMAKER DUSTIN HOFFMAN, ON PREPARING FOR HIS ROLE IN *TOOTSIE*
>
> *"Obviously you never found out."*
> — MR. BLACKWELL

The honeymoon was over as far as Princess Diana was concerned. Joining her royal predecessors Margaret, Anne, and the Queen, Diana hit the List in a big, bold splash, sinking all the way to the number one spot. In 1982 Diana was still valiantly searching for a true sense of style and a modern image, but the antiquated, stuffy gowns she wore before her sleek, svelte, shimmer-slink period circa 1988 looked like dressy prom clothes for a tea dance.

Dustin "Tootsie" Hoffman and Mayor Kathy Whitmire, Houston:

1·9·8·2 **10**

Look-alikes wearing Betsy Bloomingdale's discards!

The year's biggest hit film, the Dustin-in-drag *Tootsie*, caused a rash of rose-tinted sunglasses and 1950s hairdos to break out in secretarial pools across the nation. In his one big beaded bonanza, a Vegas reject from one of a thousand lounge acts, Dustin dusted the fashion floor – in electric-red sequins, yet. His alter ego in real life, Houston Mayor Kathy Whitmire, joined him for the tenth spot. Although her affinity for Reagan red was less pronounced, Mayor Kathy set feminine power dressing back to the Hetty Green era in terms of drab, boxy, boring outfits. Why did women feel a need to dress like men when they enjoyed positions of power? Heaven knows, the men didn't look any better. Mayor Kathy's desire to fit in only made her look dreadfully out. With her bows and jackets and school-marm skirts, Houston was in a lot of fashion trouble.

The second member of the "Dallas" contingent to hit the skids was poor Pam Ewing: Victoria Principal. Unlike her fashion competition on another nighttime soap, "Dynasty," Victoria was about as exciting off the set as a bar of saddle soap. Victoria took the valley look to heart, causing the rest of us to wonder when she would give up malls and start developing some fashion principles of her own. Her co-star in fashion crime, Charlene Tilton, was impervious to criticism. She only fell deeper into the abyss of atrocity that defined her look. It was enough to make you hope Miss Ellie would shake some sense into her ranch mates – until you took a look at what *she* had on. *Depressing* wasn't the word.

Television hostess Cathy Lee Crosby, of "That's Incredible" fame was, in the fashion department, as mind-boggling as her guests. A mad mix of tacky skirts, tight tops, and cheap-looking jewelry fit for a circus, Cathy Lee was a victim of exploitation, and she had no one to blame but herself.

1983

FOR THE FIRST TIME IN years, the motion picture industry was to blame for the worst fashion fad since hot pants. Thanks to producer Jon Peters – who gave us a brillo-coiffed Barbra Streisand in *A Star Is Born* – and his latest brain-storm, the musical *Flashdance*, the entire country was up to its exposed shoulders in the Jennifer Beals look. And what a look it was – enough to make one remember the mini with a newfound respect.

The *Flashdance* fiasco was a true, unmitigated fashion disaster that made women resemble a brigade of bag ladies with a fetish for shredded sweats. Just when you thought it was safe to go back into the mall, the return of the rag loomed on the horrified horizon. Specifically, the fad consisted of oversized sweat shirts, elephant-size necks, headbands, short-shorts or baggy sweatpants, leg-warmers, and, of course, the obligatory T-shirt. Each item was carefully ripped in strategic areas for that "destroyed by the washing machine" ambience. I suppose the *Flashdance* look was designed to epitomize the healthy, carefree, body-conscious woman of the eighties. The attitude was no different from the scantily clad sirens of the sixties. Despite the liberated pretensions, skin was skin, and the health-club influ-ence only made sense since the Nautilus-stuffed workout rooms were the new singles bars for a

Barbra Streisand

1·9·8·3

A boy version of Medusa!

Joan Jett

A Bronx
Pocahontas in
black leather
goes porn!

Joan Rivers

In borrowed
rags she proves
the House of
Pancakes still has
the best!

vitamin-enriched generation.
On more elegant fronts, Gianni
Versace introduced simple, classic,
tailored suits while Perry Ellis
continued his stylish preppy line
that emphasized flowing skirts,
thick, handwoven sweaters, and
silk-sashed straw hats. Gianfranco
Ferre took the layered, cluttered
Annie Hall look and improvised
using lighter, thinner material that
flowed instead of flogged, but
Norma Kamali bombed badly with
hideous sea-serpent-inspired
evening gowns that had what only
can be described as mermaidlike
flounces littering the floor. Like
a nightmare fit for Neptune,
Kamali's sheaths were waterlogged
from the start.
And then there was Armani
and the return of the blazer. The
look was fine if you were over
5'10", flat chested, and wor-
shipped *Mildred Pierce*. Otherwise, the prices Armani charged
for his little tailored tops and
wrinkled short pants were more
memorable than his collection.

Twiggy

Lady Godiva
dressed for a
Roman orgy!

Kathleen "Koo" Stark

A fashion Frankenstein
waiting at the palace gate!

NOTES of INTEREST

"Dynasty" reigned supreme in a shower of rhinestones. The biggest bitch on television, Alexis Carrington Colby, was also the pinnacle of movie queen camp, Nolan Miller-wise. Miss Joan Collins, who, just a few short years earlier was starring in movies with mutant rats, had made an onscreen comeback in the role of Alexis that rivaled Cleopatra's entrance into Rome. Suddenly La Collins was the biggest star in the ABC firmament. As the scheming, seething, snarling siren of an ultra-rich and ultra-spoiled Denver dynasty, Joan's jewels were mind-boggling. Off the set, everything about her was equally shocking, in a painful way. Her Flo Ziegfeld-inspired evening dresses, with more glitz than the Ritz, buried her in more bombs than an old Eddie Fisher résumé. Bust to the wind, and ruffled hips headed south, Collins was little more than a parody of her alter-ego at Colby Co. She hit the Chairman of the Board position on my Worst Dressed List as effortlessly as Alexis made money – and enemies. I was more than happy to join her blacklist. I always thought Krystle looked better in her "Dynasty" duds, anyway.

Like an endless series of Chinese water torture mishaps, Barbra Streisand was back to terrorize the world in her *Yentl* drag in 1983. Whether in pin-striped zoot suits, jeweled chokers that gave her that perpetually strangled look, eggbeater curls exploding, or the particularly unfortunate white chiffon fiasco (replete with Victorian lampshade spangles) worn to her *Yentl* premiere in Los Angeles, Streisand was Streisand. As tacky as ever. And, as her hymn to study proved, as talented, too. She placed number two, only because Joan Collins can't sing, star, and direct at the same time.

The rock world was represented in stellar basement fashion with Joan Jett, who looked like an usher at a rundown Pussycat Theatre – either that or Halloween came early. Soft-porn princess Koo Stark, she of Prince Andrew flame – and fame – was perfect for the Royal family. With her fashion taste, she fit right in. Queen Elizabeth's best friend, Joan Rivers, was equally horrific in her wardrobe of groaners, while Boy George proved he had more club in his culture than culture in his club. A punk caveman in drag, George pranced across the stage like a nelly Neanderthal addicted to neon rags, ugly skirts, and Susie Wong makeup. Truly too much for color TV – in more ways than one.

1983

Lauren Tewes 1·9·8·3 **7**
A shipwrecked Tugboat Annie!

 1·9·8·3 **8** ### *Donna Mills*
Yesterday's draperies from the Roxy Theatre!

1·9·8·3 **9** ### *Olivia-Newton-John*
From toes to nose, a shredded tragedy.

10 ### *Boy George*
1·9·8·3
Victor/Victoria in bad drag!

Worst
1
19 84

Cher

A plucked cockatoo setting femininity back twenty years!

1984

THE ANDROGYNOUS look – started in the seventies by Bowie, the New York Dolls, and Iggy Pop, for starters – made a big comeback in 1984. Forget *Vogue* and *Women's Wear Daily*. The new fashion bible was MTV, whose twenty-four-hour orgy of music videos featuring such gender-benders as Annie Lennox, Prince, Boy George, Grace Jones, and Diana Ross wanna-be Michael Jackson, paved the role-reversaled road for the mass unisex craze.

Leather jackets, Marine cuts, torn jeans, chain-link fence jewelry, and Third Reich black boots – simply perfect for the Junior Miss department. Outfits only suitable in dubious retreats indigenous to San Francisco were now sported by Girl Scouts in broad daylight. Truly, civilization was ending as we once knew it. The men – in typical eighties style – had found a new love and her name was Mary Kay, as in cosmetics. Michael Jackson, Prince, and Boy George had the power to petrify, while little plaid kerchiefs, so popular with the macho Springsteen crowd, were worn bandana style, reviving the sharecropper look in a sea of red, white, and blue.

In the fading world of Seventh Avenue, the Kleins were hot. Calvin's baggy wool pants, trench coats, blazers, and simple sweaters were suitably AC/DC to please everyone. As for Anne, the Queen of the Yuppies, her boring line of print skirts paired with oversize blazers, scoop tops, and espadrilles nevertheless jumped off the racks, while Ralph Lauren's country/preppy/East Hampton frocks offered everyone the ability to look as bad as C. Z. Guest without the burden of being listed in the Social Register. For the updated Carnaby Street look, Stephen Sprouse's miniskirts and graffiti-inspired prints attempted to amuse but were so sloppily executed that no one was laughing for long.

Through the storm of sexual duality, Reagan red was still the haute couture color. Galanos, St. Laurent, and Ungaro showed fitted skirts, boxy jackets, and wide shoulders – all in various hues suitable for Nancy's closet.

True creativity and panache was lost in 1984. When Clara Peller belted out "Where's the Beef?" in her wildly popular Wendy's commercial, she could have been talking about the anemic fashion industry.

Patti Davis

1·9·8·4
3

Packs all the glamour of an old wornout sneaker!

1984

1·9·8·4
4

Cyndi Lauper

Looks like the aftermath of the San Francisco earthquake!

1·9·8·4
2

Miss America (Sharlene Wells)

Looks like an armadillo with cornpads!

Oh My Goodness!

1·9·8·4
5

DiahannCarroll and Joan Collins

Two movie queens fighting for the
"tacky taste" crown of the forties!

 1·9·8·4
6

Victoria Principal

She is everyone's
"Yankee Doodle Dandy"!

Barbra Streisand **1·9·8·4**
7

The Al Capone look
with electrocuted hair!

NOTES of INTEREST

So many fashion flops in 1984 – and so few slots to slip them into for posterity's sake. Thus, for the first time, two ties were evident in the year-end Worst Dressed roundup. And believe me, it was a less than appealing sight. The first desperate duo, coming in for the couture kill in tenth place, was rock monstrosity extraordinaire Twisted Sister tying with His Royal Repulsion, Prince. Light-years beyond mere wardrobe madness, these musical discords were masters of their own trash/flash stratosphere. Since Twisted Sister had no real talent to speak of, the insanity angle of their name – and their clothes – made some sense. But Prince was a different story. The Mozart of Minneapolis, whose musical genius was undisputed, did, however, possess a very large Achilles' heel when it came to his closet. His look was very purple, very Vegas, and very schizophrenic. The fact that he was the size of an undernourished munchkin only made his boot fetish that much more frightening. He looked like a demented toddler trying on adult shoes for the first time.

Speaking of eternal horror shows, Cher had resurrected herself once again and hit the big time. In her latest reincarnation, she was Serious Actress Personified, with *Come Back To The Five and Dime, Jimmy Dean* and *Silkwood* under her Gucci belt. Her taste in film work was exquisite; her taste in clothes eternally horrific. It's nice to know some things never change. Cher and her wacky wonderland of a wardrobe were, without a doubt, one of life's crazy constants. Cher's timeless stability in picking out the worst outfit at the worst time for the worst possible event was, in our throwaway society, nearly an American tradition. They should make her a holiday – call it Halloween II.

"I look like a lot of people you might have grown up with."
– 1984 LISTMAKER SALLY FIELD,
COMMENTING ON HER MASS APPEAL

"I moved."
– MR. BLACKWELL

Not far behind in the Fashion Institute of Terror lurked Barbra Streisand – always hideous, always reliable. Newcomer Cyndi Lauper, who reminded me of a punk version of Barbra, was a psychedelic nuclear explosion in beads, bows, rags, and tattered rag-doll ruffles. Strictly out of some musical twilight zone known only to her.

"Dynasty's" Joan Collins and Diahann Carroll tied for fifth place – beautiful women in sequined travesties that parodied every chorus girl in her Saturday night worst. Hopeless.

And then there was First Daughter Patti Davis, on a par with Amy Carter. Even the White House blushed.

1·9·8·4
9 *Pamela Bellwood*
The living end of the endangered species!

Twisted Sister
A Mardi Gras nightmare!

1·9·8·4
10

and Prince
A toothpick wrapped in a purple doilie!

THE "MIAMI VICE" LOOK – for men and women – was the pastel-hued news in fashion for the trendy television set. Blazers and T-shirts, in ice-cream colored shades, matched with blousy pants in cotton or linen, no socks, and loafers, took America by storm. The fad lasted much longer than it had any right to. It was enough to make anyone with an allergy to sherbet quite unhappy, indeed. And while the no-sock look managed to epitomize the life of leisure, it is worth noting that Odor Eaters gained widespread popularity during this low-point in fashion history. A fitting consequence and a sad commentary on a hopelessly contrived fashion statement.

Stirrup pants were another incomprehensible fad in 1985. The unfortunate fact that stirrup pants emphasized an area most women wanted to minimize – the hips – only served as a warning to anyone over size 10 that Seventh Avenue was concerned only with the youth market. Everyone else was out of luck – and, sadly, out of fashion options, too. Most women had a better chance of finding suitable clothes at a thrift shop than on the racks of rags *au courant* in 1985.

The Madonna moment continued to hold America spellbound. She singlehandedly brought fake pearls back in style long before Barbara Bush made headlines with her double-stranded statements. And, excluding "Miami Vice" loafers, the Reebok Revo-

lution had hit in a sporty way, à la Cybill Shepherd's penchant for wearing them with everything from jeans to evening gowns.

In haute couture, Karl Lagerfeld, hiding behind his mysterious fan and sunglasses, summed up the dearth of stylish design in *Vanity Fair* when he eulogized that "there is no major figure, no determining style. There is no first place anymore." But the last-place spot had a waiting list that stretched farther than Donna Karan's knit mummy dresses. One expected Boris Karloff to burst out of Miss Karan's cashmere Ace bandages at any moment.

To prove that fashion wasn't all bare ankles and glorified dance wear, Gaultier showed fishermen's sweaters stretched to dress length, replete with breastplates for that Joan of Arc/Viking warrior ambience. From the mundane to the ridiculous seemed to be the uncontested rule for 1985, although the ubiquitous Reebok did enable one to flee the scene of countless fashion crimes faster than ever before.

Worst
1
1985

Princess Stephanie

Her royal unisex wardrobe entitles her to use either bathroom!

1985

1985

Joan Collins **②**

One more
pushup and she'll
have three chins!

 ③

Madonna

Skid Row's nomination for a
poverty-party centerpiece contest!

*" A lot of times I've been a
complete mess onstage, but there was
nothing I could do."*
— 1985 LISTMAKER TINA TURNER,
ON HER WARDROBE TO *ROLLING STONE*

"What's your excuse offstage?"
— MR. BLACKWELL

What Typhoid Mary was to hygiene, Madonna was to fashion: deadly. The musical sensation of the moment, Madonna Louise Ciccone was a 1980s version of vamp queen Theda Bara, blonde temptress Marilyn Monroe, and the Fredericks of Hollywood brassiere model, all rolled up in one stupefying package. Madonna danced and bleated her way into the MTV'd souls of teens everywhere. They emulated her grotesque mix of dimestore crosses, fingerless gloves, lacy lingerie, and moussed grease-monkey tresses right down to the beauty mark on her chubby cheek. Like quicksilver – or quicksand – Madonna jumped from one Melrose Avenue fashion trap to another – a masochistic chameleon with one constant: every look she assumed was a lesson in lunacy. To paraphrase Mae West, Madonna's taste was as pure as the driven slush.

The David Bowie of the royalty circuit, Princess Stephanie was built like a San Franciso 49'er – and dressed to prove it. She didn't need her own bodyguard; looking at her dressed in unisex leather and "Star Trek" coiffure was enough to clear the room once and for all. Rumor had it Stephanie was lonely and needed attention. Her wardrobe caused both problems simultaneously.

4

1·9·8·5

Tina Turner

Some women dress for men . . . some dress for women . . . some dress for laughs!

Michele Lee

Looks like King Kong's mother-in-law. Thank heaven spring has sprung; now she can wear a lighter shade of black!

Whoopi Goldberg

A cover girl for the *Sharecropper's Monthly!*

Cybill Shepherd

Fashion's number one embarrassment – sneaky sneakers and a plunging neckline. Looks like a turkey on its way to slaughter!

A reject from the Shah's harem. Now she can remake Scheherazade! Hair by Spikey.

Living proof that every prince needs his jester. Big Bird bites the dust!

NOTES of INTEREST   1985

The cavewoman of rock and roll, Tina-the-Twister-Turner had enjoyed a fabulous comeback, sans old nemesis Ike. Her new nemesis was a penchant for rag dresses and spike heels, fishnet hose, and streaked fright wigs. "What's Taste Got To Do With It?" Don't ask La Turner; she's made a career out of impersonating Jungle Jane.

The queen of the cul-de-sac, "Knots Landing's" Michele Lee had competition with co-star Lisa Hartman for Worst Dressed nighttime soap star – both were wipeouts in the worst way. Michelle was a symphony of black knit while navel-baring Lisa made Madonna look like Loretta Young. Joan Collins edged them out – something to do with more experience, I suspect.

An exploding overstuffed cabbage!

Whoopi Goldberg was thrilled when she heard she made the List. Believe me, I was only doing my job. Whoopi was Harpo Marx in dreadlocks, smock, and Reeboks. Like Harpo, everyone else was speechless, too.

1986

AS A REACTION TO THE eclectic, complicated, messy fashions of 1985, the fashion trend of 1986 was blue-blooded WASP – the simpler the better. The dressed-down, understated look offered little room for improvisation but was, nonetheless, a welcome respite from the spangled, circusy wardrobes that had pummeled good taste to the ground for years. Anything *nouveau* was out. Antique jewelry (if not from Grandma's private collection, then from estate auctions at Sotheby's), cashmere sweaters, skirts, and suits were typically understated and ultra-elegant. Discreet diamonds, old gold, and real pearls separated the Philly mainliners from the urban Madonnas. No-nonsense hair, with that just-off-the-polo-field feel – swept back with bows and tortoise-shell barrettes – were classic Country Club and just boring enough to pass Social Register approval. Everyone's favorite gardener, C. Z. Guest, introduced a luxurious line of cashmere knitwear in tons of white, the old-money glamour color, while the more adventurous fell for Oscar de la Renta's off-the-shoulder, big-bowed silk extravaganzas. So perfect for the Met opening, don't you know.

The big new couture hope was Azzedine Alaia – the darling of the moment in the revolving-door

Meryl Streep

A gypsy abandoned by a caravan!

19 ▲ 86
①
Worst

syndrome of fashion fame. Alaia was, no doubt, extremely talented, with a fabulous sense of high drama, rich, luscious color, and stunning style. But his contour-hugging deluxe body wraps, which fit the body like a second skin, were better suited for Amazons like Grace Jones than the average American consumer. Azzedine topped his smooth sheaths with elaborate draped hoods that blended the Mother Superior attitude with Little Red Riding Hood's whimsy. Not your typical PTA meeting garb, but infinitely more interesting and eye-catching than Donna Karan's similar collection, which paled in comparison.

Vanna White

Fashion's booby prize of the year!

Sarah, Duchess of York

Looks like the queen of last year's English county fair!

Bea Arthur

Wears all the leftovers from a marked-down garage sale!

Blue jeans, T-shirts, Reeboks, and leather jackets continued to annoy, while the pink-lipped attitude, circa 1965, was back to remind us the Twiggy look was not a buried fad. Halter dresses were hot again, too – women were busting out all over in their supposedly sexy tops, looking more like go-go dancers than glamour girls in their barely there bombs.

1986

1·9·8·6
5
*Tyne Daly and
Sharon Gless*
Fashion frumps of the year!

1·9·8·6
6
Barbra Streisand
A shoddy Second-Hand Rose looking for a
tour guide in Brooklyn!

As a newcomer to the List, Miss Meryl Streep needed to concentrate less on perfecting accents and more on perfecting her fashion sense. Marvelous Meryl, surely one of the greatest actresses ever to grace a screen, was the year's biggest fiasco in garish gypsy garb, stringy, shapeless hair and flea-market jewelry Ali MacGraw wouldn't even want. On the silver screen Streep was impossibly elegant; off the screen, just impossible. Too much method in her work and not enough in her closet catapulted her to a position she was accustomed to: number one.

The latest blight on the royal family, Prince Andrew's new bride, Sarah Ferguson, fit in frightfully well with the endless assault of mundane frocks the royals refused to relinquish. Sarah – more the Duchess of Disaster than the Duchess of York – was Central Casting's perfect milkmaid, awash in checks, frumpy smocks, unkempt Orphan Annie-red hair, and boxy school marm shoes. Only her radiant smile managed to emerge unscathed by her very unregal fashion attitude.

Television's new vowel queen, Vanna White, was a rotating wheel of misfortune in her seventies cocktail lounge singer getups, in colors like aquamarine and kelly green. Although Vanna flunked fashion, she was perfect for a remake of *Valley of the Dolls*. The studio wouldn't have to spend a cent on costuming Miss White; her closet could easily provide enough sex-siren catastrophes for a dozen sequels.

Supersensuous Kathleen Turner, who wowed America in *Body Heat*, chilled fashion observers to the bone in her too-tight, too-cluttered, too-tacky gowns, while Jean Kasem, wife of Casey Kasem, proved exhibitionism wasn't dead. Jean, wearing the most outlandish outfits this side of Saturn, was beyond description. Her lack of taste was exceeded only by her penchant for publicity. She knew a lot about top ten lists; hitting the final spot on mine was an honor she truly deserved.

Perennial favorites Barbra Streisand and Cher were back again – as gaudy and as gauche as always – while Bea Arthur, the original gender-bender from "Maude" who immortalized the Miami matron look with her print smocks and tunic tops, looked more like a policeman in drag than ever before – with sincere apologies to the men in blue.

1·9·8·6 **7** *Kathleen Turner*

Some people paint by numbers; Kathleen must dress by numbers, but obviously lost count!

1·9·8·6 *Cher* **8**

Popular Mechanics Playmate of the month. Someone must have thrown a monkey wrench into her fashion taste!

Whoopi Goldberg

Whoops! Running for the leader of the
bag ladies from Ash-can Alley!

Jean Kasem

Looks like a
wrinkled toothpaste
tube exploding!

> "*I dropped all the way to Number Nine? I must have pissed him off.*"
> – 1986 LISTMAKER
> WHOOPI GOLDBERG, ON
> FINDING OUT SHE MADE
> THE LIST TWO YEARS IN
> A ROW
>
> "*I never get mad – I get even.*"
>
> – MR. BLACKWELL

Lisa Bonet

Dracula's idea of a good time!

WHAT HELL HATH the physical fitness craze wrought? Spandex was everywhere, like a particularly unsettling invasion of body-snatchers addicted to rubberized rubbish. Spandex was the eelskin of choice for biking shorts, skirts, even skintight evening dresses. Like double-knit in the 1970s, Spandex was hideous at best.

Other dubious fads of 1987 included washed-out denim – and, God knows, it was. Fundamentalist queen Tammy Faye Bakker brought back the trowel to apply her *Cabaret*-like eye makeup. Tammy's rhinestone ensembles made K-Mart look like Bergdorf's and her prewashed pantsuits were, alas, too typical of mass American dressing. Completely insufferable.

From the ridiculous to the sublime, Tiffany celebrated its 150th anniversary. Star designer Elsa Peretti's elegant silver creations proved to be bigger, bolder, and better than ever. Designer Thierry Mugler actually introduced a beautiful empire dress with a slim, ruffled skirt that proved there was still a shred of hope. But, then, like a Parisian version of Mount St. Helens, along came Christian Lacroix to create a new fashion look – strictly for the cartoon set with money to burn.

Lacroix was the current darling of *Women's Wear Daily*. But there was just one insurmountable problem: no one could really wear his operatic opulence without police protection. Huge quilted skirts, garish toreador wraps, neon-colored jackets, birdcage hats, and $200,000 embroidered sable coats typified his outlandish, campy, and explosive collection. Lacroix's fashions were rigid, stiff, and cost more than most Third World countries' national debt. Enough is enough.

Legendary couturier Valentino made a big American comeback in 1987, and his flouncy, glamour silhouettes were manna from fashion heaven after the excesses of hyped-to-the-max Lacroix.

1987

The number one worst-dressed woman of the year was Lisa Bonet of "The Cosby Show." As Denise Huxtable, Bonet was a small screen sensation. Off the set, she was a bundle of tattered chiffon skirts, lace bra tops, Medusa ringlets, bare feet, and omnipresent nose rings. No doubt Ms. Bonet had God-given comedic talents – each appearance was more unintentionally hilarious than the last. In essence, she was little more than a road show verson of Prince – with a sixties Bohemian complex. The NBC peacock blanched, America collectively gaped, and I reacted accordingly.

Ten years after Diane Keaton started the *Annie Hall* look, the eccentric star was still living in layers, layers, layers. Messy wasn't the phrase. Diane resembled a wash-and-wear hurricane *ad nauseam*. Her inspired performance in *Crimes of the Heart* was nothing compared to the crimes of the closet she stunned the nation with.

②
1·9·8·7
Diane Keaton
A bag lady after winning the lottery!

③
1·9·8·7
Justine Bateman
A painfully stuffed sausage, unmercifully squashed in a tired old Esther Williams bathing suit!

1·9·8·7
④
Cyndi Lauper and Cher
Minsky's rejects, still trying!

Appearing at the Emmy Awards in a Spandex bathing suit, Justine Bateman of "Family Ties" proved you can take the girl out of the Valley but you can't take the Valley out of the girl. Justine has about as much style as a bowling alley, and dresses to prove it.

In a tie for fourth place, the plucked cockatoo contingent was represented in frightening fashion by Cher and Cyndi Lauper. Cher, who had emerged as one of Hollywood's best actresses with such films as *The Witches of Eastwick*, *Suspect*, and *Moonstruck*, was suffering from sunstroke when it came to her wardrobe. Cyndi Lauper, desperate for attention now that Madonna had usurped her position as the most popular female artist of the year, was an absolute embarrassment. Her highly publicized interest in the sport of wrestling made perfect sense. She looked like the wrestling mat after one too many "Wrestlemania" freak shows.

⑤
1·9·8·7

Princess Stephanie

A gender-bender fashion frump -- heaven help the Monarchy!

⑥
1·9·8·7

Shelley Long

From toes to nose, a comedy of errors!

"Dynasty's" Joan Collins, who had spent a lifetime being compared to Elizabeth Taylor, now had the distinction of looking worse than Taylor. With huge ruffled skirts that accentuated all the wrong bulges, low-cut evening disasters that would have embarrassed Mae West, and Cleopatra makeup, Joan was as stylish as an overstuffed scarecrow.

Princess Stephanie continued her macho Levi and leather look while newcomer Meg Ryan, star of *D.O.A.* was dead on arrival fashion-wise, as well. Sally Kellerman managed to resemble a butch version of Christine Jorgensen and Shelley Long emphasized the 1940 librarian at large look in her too prim, too proper preppy drag.

> *"Michelle Pfeiffer is so pretty, but the way she dresses, it's horrid."*
> – 1987 LISTMAKER JOAN COLLINS, ON FASHION IN *TV GUIDE*
>
> *"Talk about the pot calling the kettle black . . . and besides, at least Michelle Pfeiffer can act."*
> – MR. BLACKWELL

⑦ *Joan Collins*

1·9·8·7

Dressed to chill – should be playing Baby Jane in a rib joint!

1·9·8·7
8

Sally Kellerman

A bad drag before surgery!

1·9·8·7
9

Meg Ryan

Dainty Meg -- the rag-bag doll of the year!

1·9·8·7
10

Sonia Braga and Susan Sullivan

Fashion disasters of the shah's harem!

Worst

1
19 88

Sarah, Duchess of York
The palace milkmaid strikes again!

1·9·8·8 | 2
Imelda Marcos
An over-the-hill actress auditioning for Evita!

Debra Winger
1·9·8·8 | 3
Winger gives fashion the finger!

1988

1·9·8·8 | 4
Madonna
Helpless, hopeless, and horrendous!

1·9·8·8 | 6
Shirley Temple Black
From the "Good Ship Lollipop" to the *Titanic*, nonstop!

Marilyn Quayle
1·9·8·8 | 5
A 1940s unemployed librarian!

Good Grief!

THE "IN" COLOR was lime green. Visions of Linda Blair in *The Exorcist* sprang to mind more than once. Since very few women looked good in "sublime lime," as the fashion mags hard-sold, the joke was on the bird-brained consumer. Another unsettling catch phrase began to appear: "white collar denim." White collar crime was more to the point. Denim was dressed up in a variety of colors and styles, but it was still denim, and still as dull and over-done as always.

As a welcome reaction to the recent fashion night-mares perpetrated by such egoists as Lacroix and Gaultier, ultra-feminine fantasies were back and more elegant and striking than ever. Scaasi, Lagerfeld, St. Laurent, and – believe it or not – Emanuel Ungaro all showed more than one superfeminine, dazzlingly dramatic gown that surprised everyone, most of all me. Black lace was the fabric of choice: very stylish, swank, and seductive.

Sleek, chic, simple, unclutter-ed hair was also enjoying a welcome revival. The look was strictly Alexandre de Paris – all slick chignons, hairpieces tied with bows, sculpted swirls, and pony-tails for evening, accenting pale, pale skin. Tanning was out – now and forever.

Along with the good news comes the bad. Besides the parade of grasshopper-colored fashion vic-tims, the tie-dyed look reared its multihued head. T-shirts, shorts, pants, and skirts were put through the wringer, ending up looking like Peter Max's dropcloth.

Since American fashion was at a standstill, Seventh Avenue looked to Africa, Egypt, India, and Bali for inspiration. Kufi hats, shawls, Egyptian prints, Bali batik, and Indian cotton were hot for spring. Colors were crayon-bright, bold, and entirely too cluttered for anyone beyond pre-school pubescence. The mad gypsy getups that took the summer by storm were some of the worst mix-matches this side of Transylvania.

Always one to stun, Norma Kamali brought out a line of stuffed-sausage dresses that managed to set female sexuality back to pre-Mansfield days, while city shorts, supposedly the height of urban daywear chic, were more *Huckleberry Finn* than anything else. Mark Twain would have loved the look – and that's about it.

1·9·8·8

⑦

Lisa Marie Presley, Carrie Hamilton, and Katie Wagner

A trio of fashion terrors!

⑧

Jamie Lee Curtis

A pin-up for Second-Hand Sadie's Thrift Shop.

1·9·8·8

1·9·8·8

⑨

Jodie Foster

"Accused" of flunking fashion. Guilty as charged!

NOTES of INTEREST

Since her marriage to His Royal Teeth, Prince Andrew, the Duchess of York had bounced from cold to hot to cold in British popularity polls. In the fashion department, Sarah had real stability: she was perpetually dressed for the barnyard in Little Miss Muffet rags that only grew more juvenile as she got older. Even Princess Margaret – infamous for wretched taste extraordinaire – paled in comparison.

Speaking of the monarchy – or lack thereof – exiled Imelda Marcos was her outrageous worst in 1988, showing up at a New York courthouse in aqua chiffon and beehive bouffant – in the broad daylight, no less. Jaded New Yorkers cleared the streets quicker than it took Mayor Koch to style his hair – ten seconds, tops.

Madonna went the torn-jeans route in 1988. Whatever pseudo-glamour she possessed was lost in a desert of denim and dark, dye-damaged hair. Madonna's big career move centered around her hyped Broadway debut in David Mamet's *Speed the Plow*. She looked as if she had spent her life behind one.

The blue-collar comedy queen, Roseanne Barr, reminded me of Rosey Grier – post skin and sex change. The football jerseys, polyester pants, and steroid-sized shoulder pads were more suitable for the Wide World of Sports than the Wide World of Roseanne. And about that end zone! Cities have been erected on less space.

Marilyn Quayle, not one to take fashion attention away from her Dapper Dan, took dowdy to heretofore uncharted depths in her too bland, too boring suits and shapeless dresses. To top off her funeral parlor charisma, the pained expression she constantly wore throughout the year was perfect for a Preparation-H ad. An homage to horror if there ever was one.

In a ménage à trois of fashion tragedy, star daughters Lisa Marie Presley, Carrie Hamilton, and Katie Wagner tied for seventh place. The viper's nest of punk/funk/trash/flash these lost souls stunned the nation with was a deadly mix of too much money and not enough taste.

Debra Winger was proud of the fact she refused to play by the rules – and her wardrobe proved it. She'd be perfect for a Ma Kettle remake – if, in all honesty, Ma Kettle ever looked this bad.

1·9·8·8
⑩

Roseanne Barr

Fashions by Goodyear, body by Sara Lee!

LEGENDARY ORACLE OF fashion Diana Vreeland died, leaving an unfillable void in the world of haute couture. In a styleless society that revels in ripped jeans, torn tank tops, Lycra running shorts, and stained sweatsuits, Vreeland's editorial vision, versatility, and verve will be sorely missed. One can already imagine La Vreeland redecorating heaven in her favorite Chinese red.

Despite Vreeland's passion for red, the color of the year was decidedly drearier: black, black, and more black — perhaps in a misguided homage to the movie of the year, *Batman*, which unfortunately spawned the fashion fad of the year: batclothes and bataccessories. Quicker than you can say "Caped Crusader," a veritable batcave of merchandise hit the streets and cul-de-sacs of America. T-shirts, sunglasses, bomber

jackets, and junky jewelry sported the omnipresent batlogo; with its black and bright yellow design, the army of batfans looked more like out-of-shape bumblebees than Bruce Wayne's alter ego.

The revolving wardrobes of White House fashion changed considerably in 1989, as Bush Blue replaced Reagan Red as the hue of choice on Pennsylvania Avenue. Mrs. Bush proved one doesn't need an astrologer – or a million dollar couture budget – to start a hot new fashion trend. Her beautifully tailored, classic suits, and strands of pearls did it for her. The new First Lady, with her no-nonsense, down-to-earth look, promised a kinder, gentler fashion statement: simplicity is in, overstated extravagance is out . . . at least until the next election.

In the rarefied world of haute couture, such level-headedness was tragically absent. Lacroix perpetrated hideous clownlike bell bottoms on his fawning acolytes, Romeo Gigli introduced a $38,000

at worst. Marc Jacobs, in his hyped debut as Perry Ellis's new designer, bet heavily on satin down-stuffed vests, white fringe skirts, and neon flag-striped evening tubes. He lost big. In the shoe department, suede boots were a must, unless of course you preferred the overdone aerobic look and donned LA Gear sneakers to grocery store and opera opening alike. Only a few designers shunned fads and fancy, and presented feminine, flattering, and fabulous collections – the always elegant Oscar de la Renta, Valentino, and California's own Michael Novares, whose regal gowns rival the best Paris has to offer on any given collection. And so – regretfully – the decade boasted too few Novares's and too many megalomaniacs' design monstrosities. The eighties ended not with a stylish bang but with a wornout whimper. When the most enduring image of the year is a cartoon bat in flight, you know you've hit rock-bottom. Come to think of it, black was a most appropriate color for the year. The fact that fashion was dead was something to mourn about, to say the least.

embroidered Indian robe that no one would dream of wearing, and Versace's fetish for corsets managed to turn even the most elegant woman into an over-the-hill madam. Fabbri decorated his "dresses" with silverware for that touch of dinette drama, while Jean-Paul Gaultier's vinyl bondage suits were beyond description – and beyond mere bad taste. In America, fashion was hardly any better: even superchic Carolina Herrera, the designer Jackie O currently favors, introduced black velvet motorcycle jackets studded with gold SM accents. Did Mrs. Onassis buy one? I seriously doubt it. And I seriously doubt anyone else with an IQ above 30 did either.

Tailored suits, narrow pants, dark tights, short skirts, a jungle of animal print, and an explosion of cashmere poured out of Seventh Avenue – styles that were eclectic at best and jaw-dropping

3

1·9·8·9

Demi Moore

A Spandex
"Nightmare on
Willis Street."

1989

1989

Princess Anne

1·9·8·9

5

Lumpy, dumpy, and frumpy,
she's the boring bag lady of
Buckingham Palace.

1·9·8·9

4

Kim Basinger

This parading peep
show should be banished
to the batcave.

> *"I have never been what people seem
> to think a princess should be."*
> – HRH PRINCESS ANNE
>
> *"Obviously. Still, you're a perfect symbol
> for the Royal Auto Mechanics Union."*
> – MR. BLACKWELL

NOTES of INTEREST

Fashion fiascos of the lowest order abounded in 1989 as countless stars wallowed in a swamp of sordid styles. The missing-dress syndrome was a particular problem, via the terrifying spectres of Demi Moore in her Oscar bomb, Kim Basinger arriving at the *Batman* premiere in what looked like a negligee, and Cher's leather G-string monstrosity that even MTV banned. First and foremost is, without question, Demi Moore's now infamous Academy Awards "gown," which she proudly announced was a self-created fashion statement. Obviously Demi, in running shorts with half a skirt hanging down her back, sees herself as a cross between a guillotine-bound Anne Boleyn and a glitzy road runner. Bruce Willis gave up bachelorhood for this?

Kim Basinger, so prim and proper as Vicki Vale in *Batman*, shocked usually jaded LA filmgoers when she stepped out of her limousine at the film's premiere in a see-through nightgown of a dress – or should I say nightmare? Either way, Miss Basinger proved how quickly one can desecrate an image by exploiting herself in clothes more suitable for a Bangkok bordello.

As perennial as the winter slush, Cher threw all taste to the wind and sank into an abyss of leather, Spandex, and sequins – and a few new tattoos for that feminine touch. Her perpetual parade of gypsy-caravan disasters, aging rock-queen threads, and voyeuristic bodysuits was truly a sight I wouldn't wish on my worst enemy, much less an unsuspecting public.

Although Princess Anne was, to the shame of Buckingham Palace, involved in a dangerous liaison of her own in 1989 (purloined letters and

1·9·8·9
6
Emily Lloyd

A sweater girl for *Field and Stream*.

Cher

"If she could turn back time,"
she'd still be a bag of tattooed bones
in a sequined slingshot.

Daryl Hannah

The Jolly Gold Giant of the silver screen
looks like a Vegas Venus on steroids.

NOTES of INTEREST

all), the real scandal lay hidden in her wardrobe, which brought boring to new heights of blandness. Her British subject, Emily Lloyd, carried on the bag-lady tradition in frumpy sweater-girl looks that Lana Turner wouldn't lose any sleep over. Or anyone else, for that matter.

The Jolly Gold Giant of the Silver Screen, Daryl "Steel Magnolia" Hannah, traded in her prairie skirts and Woodstock boots for a gaudy look in 1989 – with equally dreadful results. Miss Hannah, who ended the year posing as a vampire for *Vanity Fair*, tried hard to destroy her extraordinary face and figure at every fashion turn. Only hard-core Bela Lugosi fans found her appealing. That other golden media sensation, Madonna – and her gal-pal Sandra Bernhard, who clung to her legendary side like a buck-toothed Eve Harrington – didn't disappoint in the fashion disaster department. Their retro-sixties rags – fingerpainted jeans for night, T-shirts for day – epitomized the bankrupt state of glamour in today's Hollywood, while their Bobbsey Twins from Hell act was about as original as an Andy Warhol silkscreen.

Finally, in the number one spot (the only number one position she'll ever see, believe me) is Jackson sibling and *Playboy* center-fold La Toya – definitely the black sheep of the Motown marvels. Poured into rhinestone bras, leather pants, chain-link belts, and space boots, she was truly a lounge act from Mars. La Toya made Paula Abdul's cheerleader-gone-wrong rags look positively silly by comparison. Which they were.

Paula Abdul

This fashion gypsy dances in the light – and dresses in the dark.

Madonna and Sandra Bernhard

The Mutt and Jeff of MTV: vampy, trampy, and cartoon campy.

Fashion
Fiasco
of the
Year
Award

Grace Jones

Darth Vader's fantasy in a Martian bird cage.

1990 PROVED NOT TO be the kinder, gentler design wonderland we were promised, but a Grand Canyon of fashion extremes that forced anyone with an IQ larger than his or her shoe size to doubt the sanity of style and the future of fashion. The big news on Seventh Avenue was the return of the dress. After years of wallowing in a wasteland of pants, the one-piece dress parade began its march on a gullible nation. Normally, I would have welcomed the comeback of the dress, but the 1990 looks were hardly an improvement over the peg-legged losers of the past. In fact, finding a flattering, feminine, and financially feasible frock was as impossible as deciphering the plot of "Twin Peaks." Forget who killed Saran-wrapped sexpot Laura Palmer, what American women really wanted to know was who finally bumped off fabulous fashion for good? From Lacroix's Byzantine-bomb catastrophes to Montana's unwearable atrocities to Gaultier's *RoboCop* parodies, the list of couture culprits boggled the brain. And the pocketbook. On the disaster scale, only Roseanne Barr's voice – and Oprah Winfrey's diet – compared.

By early spring, it was obvious the celebrated new spin on the traditional one-piece theme was pure Milli Vanilli: all hype, hot air, and marketing madness. We witnessed trash/flash sequined T-shirt dresses, tighter-than-tight, thigh-high tube togs, an explosion of retro-sixties psychedelic Pucci

Sinead O'Connor

Nothing compares to the bald-headed banshee of MTV. A New Age nightmare!

Ivana Trump

1·9·9·0 ②

A psychedelic scarecrow! Looks like a cross between Brigitte Bardot and Lassie!

Glenn Close

The founding frump of Nuns
Unlimited! A bad fashion "habit!"

④ ## Queen Elizabeth II
1·9·9·0

God save the mothballs; the Stonehenge of
style strikes again!

print minis that proved nostalgia isn't what it used to be, and the Ace bandagelike accessory of the moment: leggings. The Eco-chic Elite preferred the back-to-nature Grizzly Adams attire that lumbered down the fashion pike – hooded horrors dubbed anoraks, drawstring duds under dowdy duffel coats, stretch pants paired with hiking boots – all in all, simple country kitsch, with an elaborate urban price tag.

The vapid variation on the dress-for-duress syndrome was the arrival of the black catsuit – trumpeted as the fashion garment of the year. Some year! These neck-to-toe curve-clutchers were nothing more than overpriced designer straitjackets, and only managed to turn most women into an eye-popping spectacle of bumps and lumps fit for an E-ticket roller coaster ride. The fact that buyers soon discovered catsuit application required the dexterity of Houdini – and the patience of Job – mercifully doomed this leotard lunacy to an early mass-market demise.

For fall, we were inundated with trapezoid terrors – huge, pyramid-shaped coats and jackets that were especially disconcerting when paired with tights. Perpetrators of this particular style wound up looking like walking coat racks, with an off-balance fashion attitude. Accessories ranged from backpacks to bike pouches, chandelier-size earrings to spiderweb shawls, kitten-with-a-whip go-go boots to desert hip Chukka shoes. Hues like apricot, eggplant, moss, and cactus took color-code pre-

tense to the absolute extreme,
while makeup merely got lost in a
whiter shade of pale, accented by
blood-red lips perfect for that
vampy Vampirella panache.

Finally, gangster garb shot its
way into the winter blunderland of
fashion malice. Baggy suits, Al
Capone hats, Gun Moll gowns, and
mile-wide ties were donned by all
the Godfather III wanna-be's. I
thought the dressed-to-kill fashion
contingent ended 1990 on an
unusually symbolic note: in a year
of unprecedented fashion mas-
sacres, the only thing left to do was
arrange a speedy burial – cement
construction boots optional, of
course.

*"I've never met a deadline I
couldn't miss."*
– CARRIE FISHER, *INTERVIEW*,
1990

"Or a hemline, either!"
– MR. BLACKWELL

1·9·9·0

5

*Julia
Roberts*

A zoot-suit fluke –
Godfather III in
drag!

1·9·9·0

6

*Carrie
Fisher*

*Postcards from
the Edge?* Sorry
baby – more like
Discards from the
Dredge!

1·9·9·0

⑧

Laura Dern

A vision of Lust in rags
fit for a truck stop!

NOTES of INTEREST

1990

When Irish singer Sinead O'Connor skyrocketed to superstardom in 1990, even the Blarney Stone blanched, not to mention the rest of the civilized world. O'Connor, who wailed like she'd just lost her last four-leaf clover, was definitely down on her Emerald Isle luck in the fashion sweep-stakes. Draped in punk-monk monstro-sities, shapeless sacks, and mutilated jeans, and sporting a tattoo on her shaved noggin, the bald-headed ban-shee of MTV did her New Age Kojak-in-drag impression to petrifying effect. Absolutely hopeless and uniformly horrendous, O'Connor flew straight to number one in the Worst Dressed stratosphere because, newcomer or not, "Nothing Compares 2 U."

On the opposite end of the spectrum loomed diamond-drenched Ivana Trump, who, after dumping The Donald, turned herself into a sixties sex bimbo fashion fantasy, replete with assault-by-eggbeater Bardot coiffure and neon-bright mini mishaps. And by participating in the biggest fashion bust of the year (the now-infamous $200,000 Lacroix travesty unveiled at the Carousel Ball), Ivana proved once and for all that the road to fashion ruin is paved with excess upon excess. More Vegas than Versailles, Trump took the number two spot, with Close competition from a gal called Glenn.

Glenn Close spent much of 1990 lost in black sacks, burying her patrician polish in a somber sea of dowdy, dumpy dreck. Whether wrapped like a grim-faced mummy in Queen Gertrude getups or affecting a nun on the lam look in duster coats and midi skirts, Close experienced a shocking real-life Reversal of Fashion Fortune. Brilliant Kathy Bates must be Norman's long-lost cousin. After terrorizing James Caan onscreen in *Misery*, she took the title seriously and terrorized America at large in a stream of miserable boxy black ensembles and tacky sparkle sweaters. Bates accentuated the negative and downplayed the positive in her reign of fashion fear, much like Carrie *"Postcards From the Edge"* Fisher. Her writing may have sparkled on the page, but her lousy fashion image put me in a rage.

The *Pretty Woman* of film fame, gorgeous Julia Roberts, desecrated her beauty by chopping off her hair, dressing in gender-bender bombs, and wallowing in a mire of thrift shop markdowns. In beyond-baggy zoot-suit flukes, suspenders, and giant cordovans, Roberts robbed the Bank of Fashion Disaster down to the last pitiful penny. If Julia's image account was riding on zero, then catastrophic Kim Basinger was definitely overdrawn. In "I Dream of Jeannie" headbands, Barbie Doll hairdos, Hell's Angels motorcycle jackets, tired black tights, and

1·9·9·0 ⑨ Kathy Bates

Get the sledgehammer. Put this fashion fiasco out of her *Misery!*

Barbra Streisand 1·9·9·0 ⑩

What can I say? Yentl's gone mental!

I can't believe it!

bombastic boots, Basinger batted her way into the loser's circle effortlessly. And what does one say when confronted with a sight like Laura Dern? She may have been "hotter than Georgia asphalt" in *Wild at Heart*, but her wacky wardrobe left anyone with a sense of sanity cold as ice. Truly, a David Lynch nightmare with no end in sight.

Perennial potshot recipients Queen Elizabeth II and Barbra Streisand rounded out the Top Ten terrors. These two fabulously wealthy, powerful, and legendary women seem to have it all except a taste for timely, terrific fashion. The Queen, bogged down in frumpy frocks and geranium-planter hats, rivaled Stonehenge in the prehistoric ruin category, while La Streisand went the Brooklyn bag lady route in oversized rubbish fit for Bellevue. Yes, Yentl went mental, as did the other nine fashion victims who turned up on 1990's Worst Dressed List. And while fame may be fleeting, these hymns to horror can rest assured their freaky fashion mistakes will be remembered forever.

Fashion Fiasco of the Year Award

Debbie Allen

A hymn to high-tech horror! 1·9·9·0

The Top Ten All-Time

1. *C*HER

2. *R*OSEANNE BARR

3. *E*LIZABETH TAYLOR

4. *Q*UEEN ELIZABETH II

5. *B*ARBRA STREISAND

6. *S*HELLEY WINTERS

W HEN IT COMES TO SELECTING the all-time worst dressed women of thirty years of fashion fiascos, tabulating the simple statistics never tells the whole sordid story. Fashion is relative – what was outrageously shocking in the sixties is beyond bland today. After all, in the fashion disaster category, one Sinead O'Connor equals a dozen *Viva Las Vegas* vamps any nightmare of the

week. On the other hand, stars who hit the Number One Worst Dressed spot in a lean year often wound up in the bottom twenty the next. Some, after a string of appearances that bordered on boring, were "retired" from future consideration; others were bestowed "comeback status without apology. It all depended on the annual competition – or lack thereof. Still, looking back on three decades of sex kitten kitsch,

Worst Dressed Women

**7. DOLLY
PARTON**

**8. MIA
FARROW**

**9. JAYNE
MANSFIELD/
MADONNA
(tie)**

**10. SINEAD
O'CONNOR**

hippie horrors, punk rock rejects, gender-bender bombs and high-tech travesties, ten *truly* tasteless fashion terrors immediately cloud the mind. Pass the aspirin . . . unless you've got something stronger.

In fact, year in and year out, whether on the List or off, the above fashion fatalities belong to a unique stylistic stratosphere: Couture Catastrophes of the Legendary Kind. These

towering figures of thread-bare taste need no introduction: their omnipresent images just keep popping up, like stubborn weeds in a well-tended garden. So, without further ado, the Top Ten All-Time Worst Dressed Women. In a world of wanna- be's, these mythic mishaps are the real thing.

PREDICTING FUTURE FASHION TRENDS IS A LOT LIKE TRYING to guess what size caftan Elizabeth Taylor will be wearing next week – an impossibility, to say the least, even if we do hope for the most. I do think, however, that certain back-to-basic trends will blossom in a big way throughout the nineties. Now that the bangle-and-bead brigade has traded in that gaudy look for a cleaner, simpler style, fashion classicism will make a comeback, and, it is hoped, stick around for a while. Despite the coterie of couture costumers who perpetrate the circus look on gullible fashion slaves everywhere, the nineties will reject that ostentatious approach for a more conservative, elegant, and understated style. We've had our fill of "dessert" fashions; now, a "meat and potatoes" menu is more appropriate – and a lot more appetizing in the long run. When Joan Collins finally packed the last shoulder pad into her Vuitton trunk, Barbara Bush said no to Miss Clairol's Color That Gray, and Angela Lansbury became a bona fide sex symbol for the sweater and pearls set, the winds of change evolved from a minor breeze into a major typhoon.

The Nineties and Beyond

Conspicuous consumption (the different-celebrity-perfume-for-each-day-of-the-week syndrome: if it's Tuesday it must be Sophia, or is it Cher?) was a pretentious plague that hit yuppies harder than the obligatory pine nuts in their pasta with pesto. Now, entering a new decade, that Aaron Spelling existence is over and out. The BMW baby boomers – at least the ones who aren't in the slammer owing to tax schemes and junk bond dreams – will replace eighties opulence with nineties niceness, resulting in a gradual return to conservative, classic, and credible clothes that flatter without the assistance of bustiers, corsets, or wind machines. Soon, even the MTV video-clip generation will realize fashion extends farther than the neighborhood GAP and experiment with looks that last. Since their VISA's are already over the limit in typical eighties fashion, I suggest they start economizing now. When they realize today's fads are tomorrow's bargain-basement rejects, everyone will be better off – and infinitely better dressed.

Although the undying craze for fitness will continue – and rightfully so – women will grow tired of living in sweatpants and jogging suits à la Roseanne Barr and embrace a more feminine look outside the omnipresent health club à la Candice Bergen. Opulence may be out, but real glamour will always be in. Finding out what works for you (and wearing it) is everyone's fashion challenge for the nineties and beyond. As we enter a world of newfound freedom and a revitalized appreciation for individuality, fashion will undoubtedly reflect the social images of our time. A melding of cultural fashion influences will most likely dominate in the decade ahead: Oriental, African, Indian, and European styles will borrow from each other, while loose, comfortable, natural silks, wools, and cottons with subtle ornamentation will rise to the forefront of haute couture – if haute couture as we know it lasts at all. As costs skyrocket and traditional workmanship becomes unduplicatable, the grand old Parisian houses face the threat of extinction. So, too, do the self-appointed fashion dictators on Seventh Avenue, whose power seems to be fading away like the midi. Individuality breeds self-esteem and self-expression, and the women of the nineties won't be too interested in what's supposedly "in" or "out." It's time to say no to hype and yes to less. As we begin the journey, I hope the ending is a happy one. After all, we have nothing to fear but fashion itself. So here's to a beautiful decade. After witnessing the last thirty years of flops, frumps, fads, and fiascos, I *know* all of us deserve it.

With love,

Mr. Blackwell

Mr. Blackwell
1991

Index

INDEX